Shiva Sutras

Mystic Knowledge Explained

Original Translation and Commentary

By Jayaram V

Published by
Pure Life Vision LLC
New Albany, Ohio

Shiva Sutras: Mystic Knowledge Explained
Original Translation and Commentary

Copyright © 2024 by Jayaram V. All rights reserved.
Published and Distributed Worldwide by Pure Life Vision LLC., USA.
www.PureLifeVision.com
First print edition 2024
Page Count 144

No part of this publication may be reproduced, stored in a retrieval system, or transmitted in any form or by any means, electronic, mechanical, photocopying, recording, scanning, or otherwise, now known or hereinafter invented, except for quotations in printed reviews, without the prior written, express permission of the publisher or the author. Requests to the publisher for permission to print portions of this book or for bulk purchase of the book should be addressed to Pure Life Vision LLC, PO Box 1003, 102 W Main St, New Albany, OH 43054.

Pure Life Vision LLC is a registered company in the U.S.A. Pure Life Vision books and products are available through many bookstores and online websites. For inquiries, please visit https://www.PureLifeVision.com.

Library of Congress Publisher Cataloging-in-Publication Data

V, Jayaram
Shiva Sutras: Mystic Knowledge Explained
Original Translation and Commentary
LCCN: 2024940367
ISBN-10: 1-935760-15-7
ISBN-13: 978-1-935760-15-3

Printed in the United States of America
10 9 8 7 6 5 4 3 2 1
First Print Edition

To

I am grateful to all the great teachers, Shiva, Mahesvari, Vasugupta, Bhatta Bhaskara, Kshemaraja, Abinavagupta, Rama Khantasya, and Utpaladeva, who helped me understand this sacred text and its hidden secrets, and to my parents, who accommodated all my whims and gave me immense freedom to be myself.

About the Author

Jayaram V, a renowned author with a unique perspective, has penned 15 books, including Brahman, The Awakened Life, An Introduction to Hinduism, Bhagavadgita: Unveiling The Gita's Secrets, Essays on the Bhagavadgita, Selected Upanishads, Sadhana Panchakam: The Fivefold Spiritual Practice, Brihadaranyaka and Chandogya Upanishads, and Shiva Sutras: Mystic Knowledge Explained. Jayaram's insightful writings, appreciated worldwide, delve into Hinduism, Buddhism, Jainism, Sikhism, Yoga, Zoroastrianism, Spirituality and Self-improvement. He is the Founder and President of Hinduwebsite.com, a comprehensive website on Hinduism and related religions, where most of his writings can be found. To learn more about Jayaram V, please visit https://www.jayaramv.com.

Contents

PREFACE	9
INTRODUCTION	11
PART 1 - ŚĀMBHAVOPĀYA	15
PART 2 - ŚĀKTOPĀYA	46
PART 3 - ANAVOPĀYA	63
SHIVA SUTRAS – FREE TRANSLATION	126

Translation and Commentary by Jayaram V

BOOKS BY JAYARAM V

1. The Awakened Life: A Collection of Writings on Spiritual Life
2. Brahman
3. Essays on the Bhagavadgita
4. The Bhagavadgita: A Complete Translation
5. The Bhagavadgita: A Simple Translation
6. Introduction to Hinduism
7. Selected Upanishads
8. Brihadaranyaka Upanishad
9. Chandogya Upanishad
10. Think Success: Essays on Self-help
11. Being the Best: Practical Advice for Peace and Happiness
12. Thoughts and Quotations
13. Shiva Sutras - Aphorisms of Shiva (Kindle)
14. Sadhana Panchakam - The Fivefold Spiritual Practice
15. Bhagavadgita, Unveiling The Gita's Secrets

Preface

The Shiva Sutras, a cornerstone of Shaiva Tantra, have significantly shaped the Shakta and Shaiva Traditions in medieval and present-day India. Particularly, they have propelled the growth and popularity of Kashmiri Shaivism and continue to be revered as a vital spiritual text for enlightenment seekers. The sutras have been the subject of diverse interpretations, from traditional to scientific, as they view all manifestations as a cosmic energy play of Shiva and Shakti at different levels, with their union as the foundation, Shiva as the constant, and Shakti as the dynamic.

The Shiva Sutras, still a benchmark in many Tantra schools and Shaiva sects, acknowledges the play of Shiva in the field of Shakti. It accepts the duality of Shiva and Shakti in the lower planes and the reality of the world as the basis of manifestation and liberation of the jivas, identifying Shiva as the eternal, pure consciousness and Shakti as the field of Nature filled with both light and darkness. According to it, the mind and body are the playgrounds of various Shaktis. They serve as an obstacle when the beings are deluded and ignorant but grant them wisdom and knowledge when they overcome their impurities through yoga and become established in their original state, which ends with pure knowing (sahaja vidya).

I have done this translation because the sutras in this text are cryptic and contain a lot of hidden meanings. They are not easily understood unless they are viewed in a proper context and unless the readers are familiar with the cryptic tantric symbolism and concepts such as matrkas, nadis, and chakras. I have tried to provide the context, adding as much information as possible for each sutra. The sutras are useful for contemplative practice. I hope that this work will help you in your spiritual practice. I convey my sincere thanks to all the previous commentators and eminent scholars who, over these years, improved my understanding of this work.

The Kindle version of this work, published originally in April 2020, has been well-received by those who have delved into its profound significance. We are now offering its printed version along with the Kindle Version with a few changes. Some readers have expressed a desire to know the techniques to access deeper states of consciousness. However, it is important to note that many Tantra and Shaiva schools guard their practices with utmost secrecy. The techniques are typically imparted by the teachers of these traditions to their initiates according to their nature and progress. Therefore, it would be improper of me to divulge them and break the chain of confidentiality.

Jayaram V
6/15/2024

Introduction

According to tradition, the Shiva Sutras were found engraved on a stone by Vasugupta, who probably lived in the 8th century AD. He taught them to his disciple, Kallata, who later passed them on to his disciples. They eventually became the basis for the faith of a long line of teacher traditions, some of which continue to exist even today in some form. The Sutras surely formed the basis for the development of Kashmiri Shaivism, which is one of the principal schools of classical Shaivism. Each school has a distinct philosophy, teacher traditions, literature, and methods of spiritual practice to attain liberation. Vasugupta is considered the founder of the Kashmiri school, which is widely practiced in many parts of India and the world.

Kshemaraja, a pupil of Abhinavaguta, wrote a commentary on it called Shivasutra Vimarshini in the 10th or 11th Century AD. For my translation and commentary, I mainly depended upon this work, referring to its English translation by P. T. Shrinivas Iyengar, its Hindi translation by Dr. B.N. Pandit, and its Sanskrit version by J.C. Chatterji. The Shiva sutras are 77 or 78 in all. They are short and cryptic statements, which require a contemplative approach with some basic understanding of the principal concepts, methods, and practices of Kashmiri Shaivism to know their true significance. In providing the commentary, I adhered to traditional interpretations rather than trying to experiment with new ideas. I translated and provided commentary for all 78 sutras, keeping the count to 77 as I grouped two sutras into one (3.14) for historical reasons.

The 77 or 78 sutras are divided into three sections, or parts, known as unmesas. Each part points to a particular method (upaya), belief, or practice to attain physical and mental purity, clarity, and liberation. The first section is called Shambhavopaya, which refers to the attainment of pure consciousness or the natural state of Shiva by the path of knowledge by focusing upon the interluding space or silence between the two states of consciousness or two thoughts.

The second section is called Shaktopaya, which refers to the attainment of knowledge, purity, and perfection by invoking the powers or Shaktis hidden in the mantras through various contemplative, meditative, and yogic practices. In this section, the focus is not on mere physical chanting but on awakening the powers hidden in them with yogic practices through mudras and meditative inquiry.

The third section is known as Anavopaya, which contains various transformative practices and classic yoga methods, along with an enumeration of their spiritual benefits, to overcome the impurities of the mind and body and become established in the pure consciousness of the self. With regard to their comparative importance, Shambhavopaya is considered the most effective, and Anavopaya the least since it is difficult to practice due to the resistance one may face from the Shaktis.

The Shiva Sutras is a profound manual on yoga and mystic wisdom, with many secrets hidden in the coded language of its sutras as the work of Maya. They reveal themselves only to those initiated into the system and blessed with the grace of Shiva. They are useful for students and yogis who strive for spiritual purification through transformative and contemplative practices to overcome their limitations and attain purer states of consciousness. The ultimate goal is to merge into the supreme consciousness of Shiva, attaining his natural state of nonduality or oneness. This humble offering at the feet of Shiva is intended to ignite the light of pure wisdom within you, guiding you on your spiritual journey.

Shiva is found in the silence of your mind and the silence between two thoughts. The longer that silence, the greater that possibility. May you find that brilliant Lord who shines in you as your very essence, who pervades all this and is the source of all.

Translation and Commentary by Jayaram V

Introduction	14

Part 1- Śāmbhavopāya

The awakening of the Self (svarupa spanda)

The first part of Shivasutras is known as Shambhavopaya, which introduces us to the supreme state of Shiva and his unlimited powers and manifestations and how, through meditative self-inquiry, austerities, and purification of energies, we can overcome delusion and ignorance and become absorbed in him, without duality, division or separation. Absorption in Shiva imparts to a Shiva yogi the same powers and consciousness of Shiva and elevates him to his supreme, natural state of omniscience. By that, he becomes a living embodiment of Shiva. The supreme state of the pure Self manifests itself through the crevices of the mind in moments of silence between activities, and a yogi has to focus on those moments to find him and prolong them until they become his predominant state. In the first five sutras of this section, we are introduced to the knowledge of the Self, the cause of bondage, the impurity of the body, and how we can purify our minds and bodies through the awakening of the Self (Bhairava Udayma) to enter the supreme state of Shiva and become united with his powers and blissful nature. The next fourteen verses reveal the benefits of practicing Shambhava yoga. The remaining ones focus on ancillary or associated benefits of practicing it. The sutras in this section explain the immense powers and potentials that are hidden in each of us and how we can discover them and unleash them through persistent practice with the help of Shiva and bring him into our consciousness and our very being. The simple idea that threads through these 23 sutras is that by replacing your ego identity with Shiva and dissolving it in him, you can become Shiva-like, not as a theoretical possibility but in a very realistic sense as his very embodiment.

1-1 *caitanyamātmā*

Chaitanyam is the Self.

You are neither the body nor the mind but pure consciousness. The consciousness of the mind is not the same as the consciousness of the Self. It is but an impure version of the latter, formed after your birth and filled with māya and many limitations and modifications. However, it is the door through which you will reach the depths of your own being to find your true nature or your natural state. When it becomes silent, you will find the latter. Therefore, in the early stages of your practice, it is your support. No English word can fully justify the meaning of chaitanyam (liveliness) or atman (the pure Self). The atman is not a soul in the usually understood sense. The soul is more like a subtle body with distinguishable features. Atman, on the other hand, is the pure Self. It is consciousness but uncreated and without impurities. The body comes into existence because of it. The whole creation comes into existence because of it. It is eternal, indestructible, indivisible, infinite, indescribable, incorruptible, immutable, transcendental, without attributes and distinguishing features, self-luminous and self-existent. The nature of that Self is chaitanyam (liveliness). It is the essence of all and is unlimited, independent, blemishless, indistinguishable, universal, characterized by pure consciousness, knowledge, intelligence, vitality, awareness, responsiveness, power, knowing, and being, which pervade all existence in various forms and states. It is infused with the purest of energies and endowed with infinite potency, dynamism, independence, and willpower to manifest anything at will or by mere intent. Your consciousness has its force to the extent that it is pure and stable. Verily, chaitanyam is the nature of Shiva himself in his supreme state, in contrast to lifelessness and inertia, which manifest in creation when he is absent or withdraws himself. It is not confined to a place, object, world, or body but exists in all as their very Self and the highest nature. However, in the beings (jivas), it remains embodied and veiled by many impurities, whereby they cannot perceive it, know it, or experience it unless they remove those impurities and become firmly established in it through yogic practice.

1-2 jñānam bandhah

Knowledge is bondage.

This sutra can be translated as knowledge is bound (by Maya) or knowledge (other than the pure knowledge of the Self) is bondage or the source of bondage. The knowledge which exists in the Self has the same nature as the Self. It is complete, perfect, free, self-existent, pure, innate, infinite, liberating, etc. It is neither gained through learning, perception, inference, cognition, etc. nor lost by not knowing. It is always present in all whether we know it or not. However, that supreme knowledge is inaccessible to the jivas (beings) as long as they are bound to their minds and bodies and their limited existence, and their true self is veiled by māya and other impurities. It is this limited knowledge that is born from the ego and the senses, which we assume to be our own and which keeps us bound to the cycle of births and deaths. It suppresses our discernment and mental clarity and prevents us from finding Shiva, who exists in us, and from knowing our true nature or our true consciousness, which is inexhaustible and liberating. Until we succeed in dissolving it in the pure consciousness of the Self and remain established in our essential nature, we remain bound.

1-3 yonivarga kalāśarīram

The body is (an assembly of) womb class tattvas such as kala.

The knowledge that arises in the body and the body itself are both responsible for the suffering of beings. The body is made of 36 tattvas, such as Kāla, Niyati, Vidya, Raga, Kala, Maya, Buddhi, etc. They are responsible for the triple impurities (mālas) in the jivas, namely egoism (anava), attachments (pasas), and delusion (moha), whereby they remain bound to samsara and deluded. The 36 tattvas are made up of māya and instruments of māya only. Thus, the body, which is made up of them, acts as the field (Kshetra) of Nature, in which the embodied Self (jivātma) is held hostage. The body and, thereby, the tattvas are filled with different types of energies (Shaktis), which do not let the jivas become free. It is said that the supreme goddess (Parameswari), who is their source and propelling force, appears in each living entity in three primary forms: Vāma, Raudri, and Jyeshta. Vāma is the presiding deity of terrible energies (ghoratara), with which she promotes ignorance and worldliness. Raudri presides over fierce energies (ghora) and pushes the beings towards pleasures and passions through desire-ridden religious activities, thereby preventing them from seeking liberation. Jyeshta presides over pleasant energies and inspires beings to seek liberation. These three goddesses keep the bodies as their playground and the souls bound and veiled by impurities.

1-4 jñānādhisthāna mātrikā

Mātrika is the support of knowledge.

Consciousness translates into knowledge because of Matrka (Shakti). Her medium is the language. Through language, she deciphers Shiva's consciousness and reveals to us the secrets of his absolute state and how we also can attain it. Mātrka refers to the energy (the mother goddess), which is hidden in the Sanskrit alphabet (varnamala) from "a (अ)" to "ksha (क्ष)." Each basic letter (matra) in the Mātrka and its vocal sound contain a particular form of energy or aspect of the goddess. Thus, Mātrka is a force field in which Shakti, the primal mother, resides as the presiding deity (adhi devata) or the seed force (bija shakti) in various guises in all the letters and letter combinations. She also resides in the names and forms of all the objects and phenomena of our perceptual or objective reality. When those letters or sounds are uttered or when the names and forms of objects are envisioned, since space is the medium of the sound, the presiding Shaktis of the supreme goddess (Maha Shakti) who are hidden in them manifest in the space of our minds (chitta) and the space (akasa) outside. They gradually work upon the clouds of impurities in our consciousness. It is the same goddess (Mātrka) who manifests in all the words and sounds of the alphabet in different forms as their seed energies. However, the knowledge that arises from her through perception, cognition, and experience (anubhava), which is essentially the knowledge of names and forms and the objective world constitutes the inferior knowledge and the source of bondage (bandha). Since the goddesses are the cause of māya, the objective knowledge that arises from them is also infused with māya. Hence, unless that knowledge arises from an authoritative source such as Isvara, it does not lead to the experience of the subjective reality or to the liberation of beings from ignorance and delusion. Therefore, as described in a previous sutra, the knowledge of the mind and body is a source of bondage, and the knowledge of the Self or Shiva is a source of liberation. To find the Shiva in us, we have to look through and beyond the inferior knowledge and take refuge in the higher knowledge (vidya).

1-5 udyamo bhairavah
The uprising of bhairavah.

Bhairava is synonymous with the state of Brahman or the absolute state of Shiva. It is the illumination or the light or the dawn of supreme consciousness that intermittently appears in a yogi through the clouds and crevices of his consciousness as he practices internal or inward meditation on himself (adhyatma yoga), having withdrawn his mind and senses and remains absorbed in deep contemplation. Its associate power is the supreme goddess (Parameswari), the power of Shiva (Shivashakti). As the creative, transformative, and cleansing power, she cleanses the effects of māya and sets in motion the transformative process of the yogi who is on the path of self-realization to unite him with the universal consciousness of Shiva himself. Bhairava is the supreme light of lights or Brahman himself in his aspect as Parama Shiva. Its uprising force (mahashakti) is udyama. In the early stages of initiation into the path of Shiva, the yogis should envision light within themselves, or find it in moments of silence, and concentrate their minds upon it until it becomes strong enough to pervade their whole being. That light that manifests in them through visualization or by itself is bhairava udyama, the illuminated, energized consciousness, which is infused with the transformative and purifying power of the supreme goddess (Maha Shakti). When the light appears by itself and shines brightly, it is the beginning stage where the seeds of awakening are sown in the aggregates of the yonivarga kala shariram. Bhairava consciousness may manifest in initiates through yogic or tantric practice or by the mere grace (Shambhavopaya) of an enlightened guru. Bhairava Shakti is a very powerful force. She is Maha Kali, Chandi, Durga, Lalita, etc., who can jolt beings out of their animal state (pasutvam) often with a violent force and grant them a vision of Shiva. When invoked forcefully, she may also cause many deep disturbances in the body since her methods of transformation can be aggressive, angry, and violent, just as when Bhairava is active in the macrocosm as the destroyer and purifier. One should, therefore, never pull the force but let the Shakti do her work by surrendering.

1-6 śakticakrasandhāne viśvasamhārah

The destroyer of the world, wielding Shakti chakra.

Shiva, the destroyer, wielding the cleansing force of knowledge and language (or sounds, words, and syllables), destroys our ignorance and delusion. Shakti chakra is the force matrix of Maheswara or Shiva, the supreme lord in the body and the universe.

Parameswari, the supreme mother goddess, is the presiding force of it. Creation happens when he sets in motion her outward movement to the right in a clockwise direction, and dissolution happens when he sets in motion her inward movement to the left in an anticlockwise direction. Since Shiva is without a second and is pervading reality in all, creation and dissolution can happen only within him and his force matrix. That (the pure consciousness of I am) is the Self, and this (idam) which arises from 'That' is the world (jagat). The former is independent and absolute, and the latter is dependent and relative. The latter exists so long as Shiva's illuminating attention (chatanya shakti) prevails upon it and disappears when he withdraws it and goes into silence. Spiritual transformation is but a destructive process in which one has to disrupt the force of māya in the body and remove or suppress the impurities that arise from it. Success in Bhairava udayma requires visva samhara, the destruction of objectivity (or objective world) with the application of Shakti Chakra (knowledge or the use of mantras, yantras, etc.). The uprising of Bhairava (self-realization) sows the seeds of illumination, but a deeper and more destructive or transformative cleansing is required for its completion. For that, the yogi who has illuminated his intelligence with Shiva has to become a destroyer (vishwasamhara) of his own world (of delusion, duality, and ignorance) by focusing upon the illumination, which manifests in moments of silence. With practice and guidance from his guru, and countering the energies of Maya, which are responsible for the impurities in him, he has to turn inward, withdrawing his attention from the world and dissolve it in the silence of his own mind and in the consciousness, which flows from it.

1-7 jāgrat-svapna-suṣupta-bhede turyābhogasambhavaḥ

Turya enjoyment can arise in between jagrat, svapna, and suṣupta.

You can experience Shiva's consciousness in your wakeful, dream and deep sleep states also. Through effort, you can make that a continuous and uninterrupted experience. According to Mandukya Upanishad, we have four states of consciousness. Jagrat is the wakeful state; svapna is the dream state; susupta is the deep sleep state; and turya is the transcendental state of self-absorption in the pure consciousness of self or Shiva. Of them, only the last one, turya, is illuminated, nondual, and blissful. In the other three states, since Maya Shaktis remain active, duality persists. When a yogi succeeds in withdrawing his mind and senses from the world (visva samhara) with the help of the Shakti Chakra (knowledge) and illuminates his consciousness with Bhairava Udayma (awakening), he experiences the transcendental turya in the transitional or intermediate periods between each of the three states. By focusing upon that brief gap that manifests between two successive states, he lets the bliss of turya flow into him. With continued practice, he lets it percolate his consciousness and become his natural state, whether he is awake, dreaming, or asleep. The adept yogi who reaches such an advanced state of blissful self-absorption never sleeps in the spiritual sense. In him, Bhairava (the destroyer of ignorance, delusion, and desire) is awake and active. His consciousness remains illuminated with pure knowledge as Shiva's natural disposition. What sleep is to others is wakefulness for him. Even when his body and mind are asleep, he remains awake, established in Shiva or his pure Self, which never sleeps and which is unchangeable and free from modifications. Jagrat, svapna, and susupti are the deluded states of our consciousness, as we will see in the subsequent verses. Of the four states, only turya is transcendental, which arises from oneness with Shiva or the Self. In contrast, the other three arise in the field of Nature (the mind and body) and are subject to vrittis (modifications), hence inconsistent. The blissful turya occasionally manifests in them in the wakeful and dream states due to brief and sporadic openings in the consciousness. When a yogi succeeds in prolonging and sustaining it in these states also, he becomes naturally blissful (sahajananda), satisfied (trpta), and absorbed within himself. With his mind fixed in turya, he experiences oneness, whether his mind and body are wakeful, dreaming, or asleep.

1-8 jñānam jāgrat

The wakeful state is knowledge.

Jagrat, the wakeful state, is that in which the mind, the body, and the senses are active both externally and internally in their outward and inward modes, whereby the objective knowledge of the world keeps flowing into the mind from all directions. In the enlightened yogis, it transforms into the awakened state of turya consciousness, but in the deluded jivas, it remains in the impure state of egoism, desires, ignorance, and delusion. For a jiva, the perceptual knowledge gathered by the senses in the wakeful state represents jagrat. Perceptual knowledge is a problem because it is ridden with the impurities of egoism, attachments, and delusion. In their ignorant and deluded condition, beings (pass) are drawn to sense objects through desires and attachments (vāsanas). Repeated interaction with them results in attraction and aversion and desire-ridden actions. They reinforce ignorance and delusion, while the Māya Shaktis in them keep veiling them from the truth of their divine nature and confine them to their animal nature (pasutvam). Thus, from a spiritual perspective, the perceptual knowledge, which is gathered by the jivas in their wakeful state, is rather a hindrance. It may help them in worldly activities but not in their liberation. Caught in the dualities, passions, and impurities caused by the objective reality and the knowledge gained through the senses, the jivas keep accumulating karma and impure energies (Māya Shaktis) through desire-ridden actions. Shiva yogis overcome this problem through the purification of their minds and bodies. They become self-aware and introspective by cultivating detachment and renunciation, illuminating their minds with meditation (bhairava udyama), and through pure observation and witness consciousness. They let the light and the bliss of pure consciousness slowly enter and illuminate their wakeful states.

1-9 svapno vikalpāh
The dream state is vikalpa.

Svapna is not a mere dream state only. It also includes imagination or visualization. If jagrat represents perceptual knowledge which arises from the activity of the senses, svapna represents mental knowledge which arises from mentation or mental activity (vikalpa) such as dreaming or imagination. The thought formation or the flow of consciousness in such situations is without control. In that state, the dreamer is subject to duality and the distinction between the Self and the not-self. Hence, it is vikalpa (difference or bheda). In Samadhi, that duality disappears, and the yogi becomes aware of the blissful Self, still attached to the mind and body but without delusion. Hence, it is savikalpa (undifferentiated or abheda). The dream state represents the cognitive or cerebral knowledge, which arises in the mind and from the mind as thought, imagination, memory, conclusion, feeling, emotion, idea, concept, reason, wisdom, etc. Just as perceptual knowledge, mental knowledge is also limited and conditioned by the impurities of egoism, attachments, and delusion. Hence, it is also inferior and defective and less reliable as a source of valid knowledge. From a spiritual perspective, you cannot entirely depend upon either of them to ascertain truths or inquire into the nature of Shiva because they arise within the domain of Maya and are vulnerable to doubt, confusion, uncertainty, and ambiguity. However, the mental knowledge that arises from the pure mind of a discerning yogi is better, although, at times, it may require illumination from an enlightened guru or Shiva himself. Depending upon his perfection and purity, it may radiate light from within and help him in his spiritual progress through intuition. The dream states of a yogi may also reveal to him profound truths or alert him through premonition and help him in his practice. Jagrat and svapna (perceptual and mental knowledge) are helpful in the preparatory stages for a yogi to become acquainted with spiritual matters. They may also carry him to the edges of perceptual and cognitive reality and introduce him to the wisdom that arises in the depths of human consciousness. However, the transcendental truth of Shiva can be known only through turya, where the innate knowledge of the Self arises by itself without any external aid. Once a yogi attains turya, he brings that consciousness into svapna and jagrat also and experiences the continuous flow of pure consciousness even when he is engaged in actions.

1-10 aviveko māyāsauṣuptam

Suṣupta is indistinct and deluded.

Susupti is the deep sleep state, which we all experience when the mind and body are at rest or fully withdrawn and in which the means of knowing, the knower and the known are absent or indiscernible. In this state, the Self is neither known nor unknown, and the world is neither perceptible nor imperceptible. Hence, jivas do not know what happens to them in that state. This is true in the case of humans also. When we enter deep sleep, we lose all awareness and enter an indeterminate and unknown condition. In this state, Maya Shaktis remain fully active and veil our knowledge and perception. Therefore, for almost everyone, from the highest to the lowest life forms, it is a state of unconsciousness and inertia without any illumination or activity. It is also the natural condition of many lower life forms and microorganisms that lack self-awareness or sentient consciousness. Since the veiling Shaktis fully envelop the soul with the grossest of impurities, beings who are subject to it cannot discern anything. Hence, in most cases, susupti is like a temporary death, in which jivas remain in suspended animation, awaiting a new birth in the world of jagrat or svapna. However, the susupti of an awakened yogi is similar to turya, in which he does not lose his discernment or consciousness. His mind and body may go into deep sleep, but he remains awake and absorbed in Shiva, who is eternally awake. Hence, the susupti of an awakened yogi is known as turya-susupti. The next sutra explains how a Shiva yogi enjoys the three worlds without being tainted by them.

1-11 tritayabhoktā vīreśah

The enjoyer of the three is the heroic lord, Shiva.

Of the four states, the first three, jagrat, svapna, and susupti, are objective, and the last one, the turya, is transcendental. In a Shiva yogi, the three states are always illuminated by the fourth because he creates an opening and keeps nourishing himself with the bliss of turya and awareness of Shiva. Since both his separation from his impure self and his absorption in Shiva are complete and irreversible, he remains independent, free-willed (svachhanda), undeluded, and untainted in the three objective states also, whether he enjoys them or not. The resplendent turya keeps washing away any traces of darkness which may manifest in them. Unlike the ignorant jivas, the awakened one is not controlled by the veiling, māya-Shaktis who promote the impurities of animal nature and enjoy them as their food. Therefore, with his mind and body firmly under his control and free from the influence of veiling Shaktis, he keeps enjoying the three states with the illumination from the fourth. As the enjoyer of turya (turyabhokta), he remains established in the supreme state, even while he is active in the world. With his consciousness illuminated by the light of pure consciousness (chitprakash), enjoying the bliss of turya (turyatmak anandamayi) and controlling the Maya-Shaktis who are now united with him, he becomes Viresa, the lord of the senses and of the field of Prakriti. As the omniscient lord of all states and spheres and firmly united with the force matrix (matrka chakra), he remains pure even while moving in the impure states.

1-12 vismayo yogabhūmikāh
Wondrous, the states of yoga.

In the early stages of experiencing oneness with the Self in the turya, which does not last for long and which repeatedly and intermittently keeps happening, the yogi becomes filled with moments of wondrous joy. Since they are new to him, and since he never experienced them before in his wakeful or dream states, he is constantly surprised by their novelty and variety. However, since he is detached, he takes them in his stride as the play of Shiva without being overwhelmed by them. It is where he is introduced to the mysteries of mystic wisdom and the otherworldly bliss of pure consciousness that arises in him from his indistinguishable absorption into the limitless self, with the promise of more to come. At the same time, he also experiences the awakening of the Kundalini Shakti, which is locked up in the chakras of his body, and the rush of its force along the spine like an unstoppable electric current. These experiences spontaneously arise in him, irrespective of whether he practices specific yoga techniques or not. Having been blessed by the touch of Shiva or the grace of his guru, he is now ready for the adventure of a lifetime in the transcendental realm, in which his Shaktis become his partners rather than his adversaries, who now take over all the functions in his body and serve him as they serve Shiva. Liberation is a process of losing and discarding until one reaches a stage where nothing can further be discarded. Therefore, the purpose of yoga is not to gain anything but to lose all, including one's name and form and, in the final stages, the body itself. A yogi is supposed to discard every material thing he possesses. He is unlike worldly people who engage in desire-ridden actions and thereby accumulate objects and energies that keep them bound. Instead of exploring the world in search of fulfillment, he digs deep into himself, renouncing every temptation, gift, or distraction that comes his way, until he realizes that vast treasure, which lies deep within himself as his pure and resplendent self, which is free from all the limitations that are common to the beings in their physical state.

1-13 icchā śaktirumā kumārī

Uma Kumari is Iccha Shakti (the power of desire).

Kumari is a virgin goddess or a pure Shakti. She represents the unmarried or unbound power in the body or the field of Nature. Hence, according to the tantra tradition, she is not to be treated or enjoyed as an object of pleasure but adored and worshipped as an object of veneration with a pure mind and heart. In the body, she represents the power of desire (Iccha Shakti). Hence, the cardinal rule is that one should not pursue desires for selfish or worldly enjoyment. If you do it, you will violate a very important precept of Dharma and incur a great sin. However, in worldly life, we see that people misuse their Iccha Shakti to fulfill their selfish and egoistic desires. They engage in desire-ridden actions and fall into sinful ways. When they misuse their Kumari Shakti in this manner and accumulate sinful karma, they suffer from the twin evils of delusion (ku) and death (mari), which keep them bound to the cycle of births and deaths. This does not happen to the yogi who excels in Shāmbhava yoga. He knows the power and the auspicious nature of Iccha Shakti and renounces desires and desire-ridden actions. As he withdraws into himself to inquire into the nature of his true Self, Kumari Shakti causes neither delusion (ku) nor death (mari) in him but becomes the destroyer (mari) of his delusion (ku). When he becomes pure and Shiva-like through self-realization, his enjoyment arises from his natural and blissful turya, and his actions flow from his free will, now infused with the power of Kumari Shakti, rather than from desires or gunas. The same goddess, who causes karma and the downfall of ordinary beings, becomes his independent self-will (sva + iccha + Shakti), just as the will of Shiva. Hence, whatever he desires or wills, it manifests as Uma Kumari and becomes firmly established in him as his incorruptible and indistinguishable free will.

1-14 drśyam śarīram

The visible, the body is.

Śāmbhavopāya

The entire material universe constitutes the body of Shiva. It is creation itself, which arises from him as a formation or projection. In living beings, it is a formation around the Self, which is both gross and subtle. As the field of Nature, made up of the tattvas and gunas, it is responsible for duality, division, and delusion in the beings, whereby they see the world as made of different objects and themselves separate from it. Due to the power of the Māya Shaktis, they also do not perceive the self which is hidden in them. Instead, they perceive the not-self, the body, as the true self, and the objects in the world as what is theirs or not theirs. As a result, they develop attraction and aversion, relationships, and attachments. A Shiva yogi who wakes up from this confusion sees differently the world and his own body. He realizes what the Self is and is not. Having illumined his mind with Bhairava Udyama, and having experienced oneness with the Self, he sees everything as the play of Shiva in the field of Shakti. In that illumination, the whole world appears to him as his own body, and himself pervading through it. Unlike the ignorant souls, he does not perceive the duality between his body and those of others or between what belongs to him and what does not belong to him. For him, everything is an extension of his objective reality and a part of his being only. As the all-pervading Self, he sees himself in all and all the perceptual reality (drsyam) as his own body (sariram). To see things as they are is the first step to overcoming egoism (anavatvam), duality, and delusion and cultivating discernment and nearness to the Self.

1-15 hrdaye cittasamghattād dṛśyasvāpnadarśanam

When the chitta is gathered in the heart, the seeing of the visible and the dream (worlds).

When consciousness is gathered or concentrated in the heart, one enters the imaginative or dream or dream-like state. The heart is where the light of pure consciousness (Self) shines. In Shakti Yoga, the heart does not mean just the physical heart. It is the location in the body where Parashakti, the purest energy, resides. She resides at three locations in the body: the cave in the heart region where the nadis (energy channels) coalesce, the pith of the sushumna nadi where prana-shakti gathers, and the purified chitta (mind), which is filled with the illumination of the Self. It is the brightest in a yogi who has experienced self-illumination or awakening (Bhairava Udyama) in the heart and the mind. In the ignorant beings, whose hearts and minds are filled with Maya, their hearts color their thoughts and perceptions and distort their view of the gross and the dream worlds, whereby they experience duality and separation (anavatvam) and do not realize the true nature of the visible reality in the wakeful and dream states. Yogis overcome it by stabilizing their minds in the bliss of pure consciousness (where pure Shaktis reside), which leads to their self-purification and self-awakening. In the advanced stages, they go further and realize the oneness of all reality in all conditions. In that pure state, they perceive objects and the world without duality, as if they are a part of their bodies. Instead of otherness, they perceive the oneness of all things, seeing them as being clothed in the light of their pure consciousness, which radiates from their own hearts. With that, whatever they see in the space (akasa) of their hearts and minds in both wakeful or dream states becomes an extension of their own consciousness and beingness. By merging their minds in their hearts, and with one-pointedness and becoming the Lord of all the bodies (sarva bhuteshu), they perceive both the worlds of Shiva as playgrounds for projecting their own play.

1-16 śuddhatattvasandhānād vā apaśuśaktih

By meditating on the pure tattva, the absence of animal nature.

By meditating on Shiva or the Self, the pure tattva, one overcomes the animal energy (pasu-shakti). Tattvas are finite realities or modules or archetypal structures such as the elements, senses, mind, ego, etc., with which Nature creates names and forms of the objective realm or the visible reality (drsya). Suddha tattva refers to Shiva himself. In the highest state, he is nirakara (without form), nirguna (without gunas), and niranjana (without impurities), upon whom yogis meditate as pure and supreme consciousness (shiva-chaitanyam). He is also turyatita, meaning the one who is beyond the transcendental state of turya. Since he is the purest and the most auspicious, he is known as Shivam, the sacred one. When one mediates on him as pure consciousness and stabilizes his mind in his contemplation, seeing him everywhere and in everything, he quickly overcomes his animal nature (pasu-tattva) and becomes filled with Shiva nature (shiva-tattva). It is said that practicing meditation upon Shiva as pure consciousness and finding him in the momentary silence between two consecutive movements, states, or actions of the mind is far superior to many other meditation techniques. With its continued and persistent practice, one attains not only the supreme state of Shiva but also jivanmukti, liberation from the impure tattvas while still living in the mortal body.

1-17 vitarka ātmajñānam
By contemplation, knowledge of the Self.

Knowledge of the Self (atma jnanam) is gained through study, self-inquiry, the grace of the guru, and contemplation. Vitarka means reasoning, deliberation, inference, belief, or conjecture. In Shāmbhavopaya, vitarka is the constant and repetitive application of the mind on the thought that one is indeed the immortal, supreme Shiva, the Self of all. Keeping that awareness alive and active in the mind through thinking and reasoning, a yogi illuminates his mind and body with radiant thoughts and weakens the hold of Maya Shaktis upon him. Knowing and remembering that one is neither the mind nor the body but the immortal and resplendent Self - this is self-knowledge. A yogi who is firmly settled in that awareness through constant practice knows that he is not only the immortal Self but also the Self of all and that it is the same Self which illuminates all the objects in the visible reality (drsya). The material world has no illuminating power of its own. It is inert and lifeless (jada). Its Illumination arises from the resplendent Self only, just as the light from the sun which pervades our world and illuminates the objects. All the worlds, beings, and objects, including the tattvas, draw their illumination from Shiva, who is the Self of all. Illuminated and supported by him from outside as well as from inside, they all exist in his luminous consciousness (chidakasa) only and shine in his light and with his light as long as he is present in them and shines upon them. Vitarka upon Shiva without duality is the same as vitarka upon the Self, and vice versa. Knowing that you are the immortal, omniscient, self-illumined, and all-pervading Self who illumines the world from within and without, this is self-knowledge which is gained through vitarka. It is actualized by drawing the chitta into the heart, controlling the mind with Kumari Shaktis, and remaining established in the thoughts of Shiva.

1-18 lokānandah samādhisukham

The bliss of the world and the bliss of samadhi.

The yogi who has attained oneness with Shiva and awakened the consciousness of Shiva within himself is no more subject to the duality of pain and pleasure. He remains blissful in all situations when he is active in the world and when he is absorbed in himself. Staying blissful in the world (lokananda) and blissful in samadhi (samadhi-sukham) and established in pure consciousness, he remains untouched by the suffering of the world and the body. Having detached himself from the afflictions of the mind and body and giving up worldly pleasures, he is continuously blissful in all the four states, whether he is awake, dreaming, sleeping, or self-absorbed. His blissful state is not diminished when he is alone or in the company of others. It continues uninterruptedly because he transcends the duality of the seer and the seen and the Self and the not-self. In the unified state, the bliss of the Self becomes his natural state. Yogis who take refuge in Shiva have the assurance that supreme bliss manifests in anyone who overcomes duality and remains firmly established in his unchanging, indestructible, blissful, pure consciousness. Knowing that the same supreme reality resides in the world and in all beings, yogis contemplate upon him as the blissful, all-pervading, universal Self and experience the indestructible state of nonduality. This two-pronged approach to meditation brings them closer to oneness with Shiva.

1-19 śaktisandhāne śarīrotpattih

With meditation upon Shakti, the ability to produce the body.

Śāmbhavopāya

The body (sariram) is a construct of Shakti and the field of Shiva, in which he resides. Five forms of Shakti are hidden in it, namely the mind (chit), the power of cessation (nivritti), willpower (iccha), knowledge (jnana), and activity (kriya). In ordinary beings, due to māya, they remain impure, limited, and weak. When a yogi meditates upon the resplendent Shiva with devotion by fixing his mind upon him, he overcomes the impurities and releases the Shaktis from their limitations. The Shakti who arises from that churning with their combined power is the supreme goddess (Parashakti) who is endowed with indomitable will (iccha), knowledge (jnana), and dynamism (kriya). Supremely pure, without duality, division, and objectivity, she is eulogized in the Tantras as the mother of all the gods and Shaktis. She is the guardian of all mysteries and mystic powers, and the supreme means to our spiritual evolution. Without meditating upon her, none can attain supreme powers (siddhis) or union with Shiva. The yogi who succeeds in invoking her within himself either by his own effort or through the grace of Shiva gains the power to produce offspring at will in whatever way he desires or create whatever physical reality or body he would like to manifest. He can create a new body for himself as a part of his self-purification, assume any form he desires, or manifest himself in different bodies at the same time. He can do it in wakeful and dream states, in gross and subtle planes, in this world, and in other worlds also. Whatever form or object he wills, it manifests. Such is the mastery of a yogi who practices Shāmbhavopaya and achieves perfection in directing his willpower through the Shakti in him.

1-20 bhūtasandhāna bhūtaprthaktva viśvasamghattāh

The power to unite or separate elements assembles the world.

By mixing and unmixing or separating the elements, the Shaktis bring the world into existence. Samghatta means assembled, organized, mixed, brought together, or kneaded into. The body and the material universe consist of many elemental Shaktis. In conjunction with the gunas, they preside over one or more of the five basic elements (pancha bhutās) of creation, namely the earth, fire, water, air, and sky. As the deluding and impure Maya Shaktis of the physical world, they play an important role in keeping the beings bound to samsara by pushing them into the mire of ignorance and delusion and reinforcing their animal nature. When a Shāmbhava yogi takes refuge in Shiva and contemplates upon him with single-minded devotion and with a pure mind and body, he develops the power to control the elemental Shaktis in him. With the power that flows from Shiva, with whom he is united as one, he becomes the Lord of the Bhutas (Bhutanāth) who can combine (sandhāna) or separate (prthaktva) the elements at will and make objects appear and disappear or act differently, or project them or withdraw them or change their very nature. He also develops the power to control his hunger and thirst or keep his body immune from disease, weakness, pain, and other afflictions. Overcoming the limitations of space and time, he can arrange, rearrange, or replace things or change the order of their appearance or reverse their natural processes and functions, see far away objects from near, or go back and forth in time from present to past and future to foresee things in advance or change their occurrence. As the world becomes an extension of his pure consciousness, he experiences all these without duality as if they are happening to himself or within himself in his infinite supreme reality. The idea of alchemy, or transforming any metal into gold, which is prevalent in some Shaiva sects, is rooted in such beliefs.

1-21 śuddhavidyodayāccakreśatva siddhih

With the onset of shuddha vidya, the lordship of chakras is accomplished.

Shāmbhavopaya results in many supernatural powers and the awakening of supreme energies as the mind and body are purified and infused with the illumination of Shiva and pure Shaktis. Shuddha vidya means pure self-knowledge or pure self-awareness, which is the natural state (sahaja) of accomplished and illumined yogis (siddhas). Since it arises from Shiva, who is the Self in all, and suddha (pure) tattva, it partakes in his illuminating, purifying, and liberating power and sets free the limited beings (ma+anavas) from their self-induced limitations. Hence, when a yogi attains the higher knowledge (suddha vidya) by fixing his mind in the contemplation of Shiva, the chakras in him become active, and he gains immense powers. Shedding their impurities, the Shaktis in him merge into his pure consciousness without duality and become a part of his will and intention. As a result, by mere thought, he (who is now Shiva) develops the power to manifest, destroy, change, or uphold objects and phenomena. By becoming all, with unified consciousness, he attains omniscience and the endless knowledge that is innate and natural to the supreme state of Shiva. With all the Shaktis firmly united in him and under his control and with indomitable will, he becomes the supreme lord (paramesvara) of the force matrix (Shakti Chakra) of the universe, which gives him limitless powers. Endowed with purity, infinite power, perfection, and the supreme knowledge of the Self, and firmly established in the Shiva tattva, he attains the supreme state of the all-knowing, all-powerful, self-aware, self-existent, supreme Self (paramātma).

1-22
mahāhradānusandhānānmantravīryānubhavah

By reaching the great lake, the experience of mantra virya.

When a yogi attains pure consciousness, he develops the power to invoke, awaken, and activate the presiding Shaktis of the sacred mantras by chanting or contemplating them. Maha hrda means the great deep lake of pure chitshakti, which is a reference to the supreme consciousness of Maheswara in an inseparable union with Maha Shakti, the Supreme Goddess. Anubhava means direct knowing or seeing, without the intervening senses, the mind, memory, intelligence, and the duality of the knower and the known. Mantra virya refers to the potency of mantras or magical chants. It arises when the mantras are chanted or remembered with the right intent and when the Shaktis presiding over them are activated and energized by the Shaktis of the pure chitta. In their highest, unified state, all the Shaktis are indistinguishable from Shiva. Since he is their husband or Lord (pati), they are inseparably united with him and follow his will. Mātrika is another name of Maha Shakti. As the name implies, she is the source of all the letters and sound forms of the Sanskrit alphabet (Sanskrit being the language of the gods and goddesses). She remains hidden in each of the 50 letters of the alphabet as its presiding deity, endowed with specific potency and purpose. When those letters are properly joined into sacred syllables, words, or chants and orally pronounced or mentally contemplated in the right manner, the presiding Shaktis of the Mātrika hidden in them release their power, which may be auspicious, inauspicious, or mixed. The power and efficacy of each mantra or sacred syllable, such as Aum or Hrim or Kleem, depend upon the purity of the person who utters it or meditates upon it. When an ignorant or deluded person chants a mantra, its power may not properly manifest or not manifest at all.

However, in the consciousness of an illumined yogi, who sees himself as Shiva or everything as himself and who is firmly united with the Maha Shakti (Matrkia), all the mantras become self-illumined and gain extraordinary powers. When he meditates upon them, he becomes intuitively aware of their hidden meaning, purpose, and potency. It is not even necessary that he has to use sacred words or mantras to unleash such power. Since he is self-illumined and united with Mahashakti (maha hrda), with the awareness that he is Shiva and all, he becomes the master of vibrations and sound forms. His words and mere intentions carry the potency of mantras or mantra virya, although, in that state, he may not feel the need to use them since he remains satisfied and absorbed in himself. He has no purpose to achieve and nothing to conquer.

Part 2 - Śāktopāya

The awakening of innate knowledge (sahaja vidya udaya)

Shaktopaya means the way of Shakti or by the means of Shakti. It refers to the practice of invoking Shakti through various methods and seeking her help in sublimating the impure energies and animal tendencies (pashu pravrtti) of the body to cultivate the uninterrupted awareness of the Self or Shiva, despite the interruptions and modifications of the mind and body. In Sambhavopaya, the emphasis is on the absorption of the mind in the pure consciousness of Shiva and cultivating undifferentiated oneness with the help of a guru or Shiva himself. In Shaktopaya, the attention shifts to the transformation or purification of the mind and body and their energies with the help of Shaktis. This section contains only ten sutras. They allude to the powers (Shaktis) that are hidden in the sacred letters (matrchakra) and mantras and how they can be harnessed with the help of the triple Shaktis, namely Iccha, Kriya, and Jnana Shaktis. For that, a guru is the means (upaya), who should be qualified and endowed with the right knowledge (vidya), purity, and intelligence. Finding a qualified guru is the key to attaining success on this path. The body is a sacred ground, the Field of Shakti, and a sacrificial pit in which one has to perform the sacrifice of knowledge to invoke Jnana Shakti and purify the impure nature to attain unwavering one-pointedness, uninterrupted by the movements of the mind and body or the flow of thoughts.

2-1 cittah mantrah

The mind is the mantra.

Mantras have manifesting power. They extend one's reach by releasing powerful vibrations that travel through space and interact with the things of the world to precipitate reality or actualize thoughts. The mind also has the manifesting power, which gains strength to the extent it gains knowledge and is pure, united, and harmonious with the Self or Shiva. Knowledge of Shiva (Jnana Shakti) increases the mind's power to manifest, which reaches its optimum when the yogi becomes firmly established in oneness. His consciousness in that unified state is as effective and capable as a powerful mantra. Just as mantras can manifest the Shaktis that are hidden in them or preside over them, he develops the potency to invoke and manifest the Shaktis that reside in him because of his inseparable connection with Shiva. In ordinary people, thoughts require effort to materialize. In a self-realized Shāmbhava yogi who has transcended the duality of the knower and the known and is ever absorbed in Shiva with uninterrupted awareness, they manifest instantly. His thoughts and words arising from his illumined and unified consciousness are as good as mantras since Shakti shines in them with her full potency. Endowed with supreme knowledge, limitless purity and potency, and devoid of the limitations of place, time, form, etc., and illumined by its effulgence, his one-pointed pure consciousness becomes an unending source of manifesting power by itself. With that, he controls the triple Shaktis and attains the ends he desires. "Mantra" means mind power or chit-shakti, which is hidden in the syllables and sounds of the Sanskrit alphabet. Chitta is the subtle space through which that power travels as thought currents. Each mantra is a vehicle of Shakti or the Goddess. She presides over it and, when invoked, guides it to the intended goal. Without her, the mantra is ineffective and weak (nirvirya). When a mantra is fixed in the chitta and constantly meditated upon, its presiding Shakti (mantra devata) manifests and fulfills its promise and purpose for which it is intended. Mantra virya becomes limitless in a Shāmbhava yogi, who transcended māya and restrained his mind and senses. With the help of mantras such as Aum, Hrim, Sau, etc., when he purifies and illumines his mind (chidakasa) with pure consciousness, he becomes the source and the personification of those very mantras. As the lord of the mantras, he can unleash, suppress, or augment their power at will.

2-2 prayatnah sādhakah

Willful effort for success.

The yogi must make a persistent effort to succeed in establishing his mind in the uninterrupted awareness of Shiva until he reaches the transcendental state. Prayantna means willful and pointed effort in which three Shaktis, namely Iccha Shakti (willpower), Kriya Shakti (right techniques), and Jnana-Shakti (right knowledge), participate in the purification of the body and the mind, which leads to absorption in pure consciousness or oneness with Shiva. Success in the effort may happen by the mere will of a guru or Shiva himself (Shāmbhavopaya) or with the use of specific mantras, mudras, and yogic practices (Shaktopaya). The use of mind-power (Mantra Shakti) is the basis of the latter practice, but it requires both skill and knowledge. The mantra given by the teacher or the mind trained and tamed by persistent concentration should be used like an arrow. Just as its accuracy, flight, direction, and destination depend upon the skillfulness of its archer, success in the use of mantra Shaktis depends upon the yogi who invokes them. It means that one has to be skillful (kriya) and knowledgeable (jnana) in the use of mantras through willful effort (iccha). Kriya Shakti is the mover in all actions and movements. Because of her only, we are filled with awareness and consciousness (chetana), and our bodies are filled with prana. When a mantra is placed in the mind and chanted or meditated upon, the Shakti that is present in it is released as Kriya Shakti. However, she participates in the act (kriya) of self-purification only when a corresponding level of knowledge (Jnana Shakti) is already present in the yogi. Otherwise, its power is quickly dissipated. Thus, in Shaktopaya, success largely depends upon the effort and progress of the yogi, unlike in Shambhavopaya, where you attain pure consciousness through the grace and will of Shiva. When a yogi is pure and self-illumined with Shambhavopaya, all the Shaktis in him dutifully follow his indomitable will since they cannot resist Shiva. In Shaktopaya, progress becomes arduous unless you have the guidance of a guru or the blessings of Shiva. The Vinayakas stand in the way until all the impurities are removed and the mind and body shine with the illumination of pure knowledge.

2-3 vidyāśarīrasattā mantrarahasyam

The power of vidya sariram, the secret of the mantra.

Knowledge is the foundation to attain the transcendental Shiva consciousness through Shaktopaya. The body of a mantra is knowledge, and so is the case with the subtle body or the mind-body. It is what we mean by vidya sariram. According to this sutra, the secret of the mantra is its body, which has knowledge as its power (Shakti) and illumination. A yogi who illuminates his chitta and mental body with pure knowledge develops a similar power and gains lordship over the Mantra Shaktis and over Iccha, Jnana, and Kriya Shaktis. The knowledge of Shiva, the mantras, and their potencies naturally manifest in him. Iccha Shakti or Kriya Shakti are not very useful unless you have the right knowledge (Jnana Shakti) to know the secret of the mantras and how they are invoked. Vidya sariram, or the knowledge body, is a reference to the body of Shiva, which has supreme knowledge as its illumination and essence. In Shiva, all knowledge manifests by itself because he is a sahaja (original or natural) yogi whose knowledge is the superior knowledge of the Self (sahaja vidya). Vidyas are of many types. Some vidyas are avidyas (ignorance) since they arise from the Māya Shaktis, whose nature and purpose are to delude beings and keep them wandering in samsara. Mantra vidya is avidya for a deluded being and vidya for an enlightened one. Therefore, if you want to know naturally or innately the secret of the mantras or the secrets that are hidden in the inner space of your mind (chidakasa), you must be endowed with the right knowledge, not the kind that you gain through study or intellectual effort, but the one which arises innately from your union or absorption with Shiva and Shakti in their purest state. When one is illuminated by this innate knowledge (sahaja vidya), in which Ichha-Shakti is stable and firmly in control, knowledge manifests by itself, and secrets reveal themselves. Mantras possess power (mantra virya) because of the power contained in each letter of the Sanskrit alphabet. That power remains hidden in its natural state. As the tantras describe, the Shakti in them is immobile (nirachara), asleep like a sleeping serpent, and unconscious. When she is churned by the power of the mind, she awakes with a roaring sound and becomes Para Shakti, the supreme power that is twelvefold (12 vowels) with 50 divisions (50 letters from 'a' to 'ksha'). When she flows through the mind as Bhairavi in the triple forms of Jyestha,

Raudri, and Amba, the sound forms of the alphabet manifest. This is the outer secret of the mantras. Their hidden secret is known only through the omniscience of Shiva. When he is awake in you, all knowledge becomes natural, self-existent, and integral (sahaja) to your consciousness. It manifests in you and reveals itself to you by mere will without any external aid or effort.

2-4 garbhe cittavikāso'viśista vidyāsvapnah

From the flowering of chitta in the womb of māya arises dreamlike indistinct knowledge.

In māya, there is an expansion of chitta due to the activity of the mind and senses, which leads to an inferior knowledge that is as indistinct and vague as a dream. When there is an expansion of the chitta (chitta vikasa) through the higher knowledge attained by uninterrupted one-pointedness, the yogi overcomes the duality and delusion and attains the indistinct knowledge (savikalpa) of the Self or Shiva. Both happen in the womb of the Maya or within the body, but due to different efforts. Garbha means the womb. In this context, it means the body or the womb of all creation, which is represented by Maha Shakti, the great mother. In her aspect as Maha Māya or Māya Shakti, her main purpose is to remain active in the womb-born (yoni varga) tattvas and keep them impure with animal nature. Since she serves the aims of creation, she fills the beings with the triple impurities of egoism, attachments, and delusion and keeps them bound to the mortal world. The embodied beings cannot easily escape her deluding influence. She is responsible for their ignorance, delusion, desire-ridden actions, egoism, indiscretion, the predominance of rajas and tamas, sexual desires, and the like, which produce karma and consequential suffering. Whatever happens to them in her sphere is inferior, limited in scope and potency, and devoid of light and purity (akhyati). This includes any mental development (chitta vikasa), the flowering of knowledge, dream experience (svapna), and any special power or siddhi which may manifest due to the practice of yoga or the karma of previous lives. Hence, one has to be wary of any development, attainment, or progress that happens in the sphere of Māya-Shakti because it is not conducive to spiritual progress. This is true in the case of Siddhis (supernatural powers) also. If they manifest in an impure and ignorant person, he is more likely to misuse them under the influence of his desires rather than use them for his self-purification. Indeed, Māya Shakti uses all such developments as a snare to push the beings further into delusion and ignorance rather than towards light, liberation, and perfection. Hence, a yogi or an initiate should not be carried away by his intellectual development, knowledge, erudition, Mantra Shakti, or mystic powers, knowing that they are the snares laid down by māya to stall his progress and keep him bound and deluded. He should focus his effort on building his knowledge-body (vidya sariram) constantly and illuminating his consciousness with the nectar of Shiva consciousness so that he is not misled by the Maya-Shaktis.

2-5 vidyāsamutthāne svābhāvike khecarī śivāvasthā

With the natural advent of vidya, khechari and Shiva state.

Vidya means the knowledge of the Self or the transcendental knowledge, in contrast to sensory knowledge, which arises from the senses (jagrat), or mental knowledge which arises from study or from the thinking and reasoning faculties of the mind (svapna). Since vidya arises naturally when the chitta is pure and one-pointed, without any blemish or imperfection, it is considered svabhavi (natural) or sahaja (original or innate). When a yogi attains vidya through the unwavering awareness of Lord Shiva, he overcomes duality, realizes that Shiva (the Self) is the only reality, and becomes absorbed in him. Unlike material or mental knowledge, self-knowledge is liberating, purifying, blissful, independent, and born from self-knowing without the aid of the mind and the intellect. Khechari refers to the illuminating sun that moves in the bright sky of consciousness. In Shaivism, it refers to the resplendent state of Shiva, brightly shining in the inner sky of the mind (chidakasam). Sahaja vidya and the boundless state of Shiva (which are technically the same) are attained through the twin powers (virya) of mudra (yogic posture) and mantra (sacred syllables). The mudra is the khechari mudra, which consists of curling the tongue and stretching it all the way back into the throat along the soft palate and touching the nasal cavity until it is firmly in place. The seed mantra, which is used in stabilizing the mind can be any sacred syllable such as Aum, Hrim, Krim, Shrim, etc. When mastery is achieved in these two practices, one becomes absorbed in Shiva and attains his natural state (avastha) and supreme knowledge (vidya). The supreme state of Shiva is described to be infinite, pure, indivisible, blissful, independent, supremely potent, and self-existent. In that state, all the impure and deluding Māya Shaktis also become dissolved in the supreme state of Parashakti, which is an inseparable part of Shiva's pure consciousness. Now, a yogi may attain vidya through effort, through the grace of a guru, or due to the progress achieved in previous lives. When he attains vidya by any of these means, he realizes that mantras, contemplative practices, knowledge of siddhas, matrka chakra, the bliss of turya, khechari, and other mudras naturally arise in him without effort, study, or practice. How Vidya may naturally arise is explained in the next sutra.

2-6 gururupāyah

The guru is the means.

Whether a yogi practices Shambhavopaya, Shaktopaya, or Anavopaya, the guru is the means. He is greatly helpful in subduing the Maya Shaktis and attaining self-control. Guru means an enlightened teacher who removes darkness from the hearts and minds of his disciples. He fills them with the knowledge of the Self and the illumination of pure consciousness, helping them in their effort to cleanse themselves and remove their impurities and cultivate one-pointedness or the uninterrupted and exclusive awareness of Shiva's presence in him and around him even when his mind and body are engaged in actions. Thus, for his disciples, the guru is the means to liberation. He is not a mere teacher in the ordinary sense and should not be equated with those who teach mundane knowledge. Being Siddha and verily Shiva himself in whom he is firmly established without duality, he has self-control (nigraha) and the power (anugraha) to transform and grant liberation. He may also pass on the knowledge and power through his teaching (shiksha) or directly transfer his Shaktis (Shaktipath) to deserving disciples and awaken them to the uninterrupted and undifferentiated (savikalpa) awareness of Shiva even in the wakeful state. Since he is endowed with discernment, he can identify those who are ripe for liberation and help them. Since he is verily Shiva like, to be in his presence is to be in the presence of Shiva himself. Having attained oneness with him and tasted the bliss of turya and samadhi (self-absorption), he remains absorbed in the pure consciousness of Shiva. Therefore, knowledge arises in him naturally (svabhavika) and inherently. Just as he embodies Shiva, he also embodies Shakti in her most auspicious and purest state. In him, all Shaktis obey his will because he is in union with Shiva. Hence, he is also very qualified to teach the knowledge of the mantras and the methods to harness the power of mystic syllables and mantras (mantra virya). Thus, a self-realized guru (Jangama) is truly the best means to attain Shiva.

2-7 mātrkācakrasambodhah
Matrka chakra is known.

An enlightened guru knows the matrka chakra and how to harness the Mantra Shaktis, which are hidden in the sound forms of speech for self-purification and self-realization. It is through him the knowledge of mantras and Matrka Shaktis is known. Matrka chakra represents the vibratory power of Shakti in the sounds which are present in the Sanskrit alphabet. All the letters in the alphabet are born from Shakti and contain the power of Shakti. She is the moving force of prana in the nadis, kundalini in the chakras, and sound energies in the Matrka Chakra. She remains hidden in each sound in a specific sound form and acts as the potency of that sound. When a sound is released through utterance, its presiding Shakti manifests and extends into the objective world through space, where she leaves her vibrations upon objects and creates ripples in consciousness. Just as the number of letters in the Sanskrit alphabet, the matrkas are 50, or 51 if you include silence also as a sound form. Together, they constitute the Shakti Chakra or Matrka Chakra, or the force field of Shiva. The 50 matrkas are divided into two groups, namely Swara Varna (अ to अ:) and Vyanjana Varna (क to ह). Both groups arise from the seven matrkas or Shaktis. Each letter carries a potency or a certain vibratory power, which arises from the Shakti, who is hidden in it as its presiding deity. For example, a and ā (अ, आ) are presided over by Anuttara and Anandarupa; i and ī (इ, ई) are presided by Iccha Shakti and Ishana; u and ū (उ, ऊ) are presided over by Unmesha and Unata, and so on. Some letters and letter combinations, such as Aum, Hrim, and Kleem, are considered highly potent because they release powerful vibrations into the atmosphere and augment the power of Iccha Shakti and Kriya-Shakti. An enlightened guru has experiential knowledge of all the matrkas. Only he can reveal the true significance of the matrka chakra and how it can be used to cultivate purity, develop mystic powers, and attain liberation. In him, the mystic syllables, mantras, and sacred sounds come to life and manifest their power in the hearts and minds of his disciples. Therefore, he is the right one to teach them and how to harness them in Shaktopaya.

2-8 śarīram havih

The body is a sacrificial offering.

You give up the body, the playground of Maya, and your attachment to it to attain the Supreme Shiva. The body is an oblation in the sacrifice of self-purification in which the impurities of the mind and body are poured into the fire of renunciation as an offering to the Shaktis who participate in it. In Vedic symbolism, the body is often compared to butter, which melts in fire and becomes an oblation. Havih means an oblation or a liquid offering, such as oil, ghee, or milk, which is poured into a sacrificial fire. Sariram means the body. In a broader sense, it means not only the body of an animate or inanimate object but also the material world itself. For a jiva who is caught in the cycle of births and deaths, the body is the proof of his existence, name and form, and his limited egoistic identity (anavatvam). It is the source of his enjoyment as well as his suffering. Because of that, he experiences liveliness (chetana), consciousness (spandana), desires and attachments, and thereby bondage. A yogi sees the body differently, knowing that he is the true Self. Therefore, he cultivates a distaste towards it and withdraws his mind and senses to remain focused uninterruptedly on Shiva, his true Self. Surrendering the mind and body and their impurities to Shiva and Shakti as an oblation to them in the fire of renunciation, yoga, and austerities - this is called the sacrifice of the body. It is a symbolic offering to cultivate detachment, renunciation, and continuous nearness to Shiva. With that offering, the body becomes purified by the seven Shaktis of the sacrificial fire, namely Kali, Karali, Manojava, Sulohita, Sudhumravarna, Sphulingini, and Visvaruci. The sacrificial offering also signifies the symbolic death of the body and the spiritual birth of the jiva as Shiva, or pasu, the bound Self as Pati, the liberated Self.

2-9 jñānam annam

Knowledge is food.

If the body is an oblation in the sacrifice of self-purification, knowledge is the food offered to Shiva and the Shaktis who participate in it and help us in our transformation. The knowledge that is offered in this sacrifice is the inferior knowledge (avidya) of the material and worldly kind, which arises from the tattvas in the wakeful, dream, and deep sleep states and causes bondage, delusion, and ignorance. A yogi has to offer this knowledge to Shiva and the purifying Shaktis and empty himself so that he can fill his consciousness with the pure knowledge and illumination of Shiva and make his body fit for the awakening of higher Shaktis who participate in its purification and transformation. By offering the knowledge associated with his impure consciousness, which keeps interrupting him when he is awake or engaged in introspection and meditative self-inquiry to Shiva, who is the Lord of Death (Kala) and for whom everything is food and to Parashakti in her aspect as Kali, he lets the light of the Shiva gradually manifest in the sky of his consciousness through the dispersing clouds of Maya. In this manner, making his mundane knowledge as food in the sacrifice of self-purification and liberation, he renders himself fit for the awakening of higher Shaktis and higher knowledge in him. By constantly offering worldly knowledge and gross material things to the Self as food, he gives up his attachments and remains pure and steadfast in the blissful turya state even when he is engaged in actions.

2-10 vidyāsamhāre taduttha svapna darśanam

When knowledge is destroyed, the seeing of the dream.

Knowledge or vidya is of many types. Some are binding, and some liberating. Some lead us to ignorance, and some to light and wisdom. Worldly knowledge leads us deep into the dreamlike play of Shiva, where we experience duality (vikalpa) and become bound to the cycle of births and deaths due to our ignorance, egoism, desires, and delusion. Liberation is like waking up from that dream and remembering the truth of oneself. When we emerge out of that dream with true knowledge and discernment, we begin to see it as a dream. The knowledge of the Self destroys our ignorance and opens our eyes to the Self hidden in us. With that, we become seers, established in the awareness of Shiva, and begin to see things as they are. With the differentiation (vikalpa) gradually dissolving in the wakeful, dream, and deep sleep states and realizing the truth of oneness, we open our eyes to the truth of our essential nature. With that awareness soaking our consciousness, we are no longer fooled by the illusory nature of our existence, the world, or the appearance of things. We see into them and through them to perceive the truth that they are snares, not the liberating truths. Spiritual wisdom teaches us that with the dawn of true knowledge, all illusions are automatically destroyed, and one settles in the all-knowing Self. This sutra suggests the same. When inferior knowledge (avidya) is destroyed, we open our eyes to the all-pervading presence of Shiva and see the world as a temporary dream, illusion, or Shiva's play. Ordinary people see the world differently with desires and attachments since they are subject to duality and objectivity. They see themselves as living in the real world with names and forms that represent them and give them the distinction they cherish. A yogi who is established in Sahaja Vidya sees that they are caught in a dream play of Shiva and do not know it yet. Because of his absorption in his pure consciousness, he may even see that as his own play. This sutra alludes to this seeing of the dream (svapna darsanam) as a dream, not as reality. When we are ignorant, we become involved with the dream, thinking that it is real, but when we are liberated, we see it from outside in a state of nonduality (Advaita) as a dream and know that it is a dream. Therefore, we remain detached, undeluded, and uninvolved.

Part 3 - Anavopāya

The flowering of supernatural powers
(vibhuti spanda)

This section describes the spiritual perfections and powers that arise when anava (ego) is subdued, and sahaja vidya manifests through self-purification in which self-effort (Anavopaya) is the means. This is the largest of the three sections, with 45 sutras, which can probably be a symbolic inference that it is the most difficult of the three methods suggested in this scripture. Anavopaya refers to the purification of the mind and body to overcome the limitations that are imposed by the gunas and tattvas upon the embodied Self (jivātma) due to māya and related impurities. When a yogi overcomes them, he is liberated in the body (jivanmukta) and becomes a pure being who is very similar to Shiva in all respects. Ancient commentators adapted two divergent approaches to interpret this section. The first one, attributed to Kshemaraja, suggests that this section contains references to techniques that are helpful in achieving specific results in the purification of the mind and body. According to another opinion, attributed to Bhattabhaskara, this section is a logical continuation of the previous two. It is not instructional or educative in purpose but informative since it suggests benefits that naturally manifest in a yogi when he attains pure knowledge (sahaja vidya) through Anavopaya as well as the other two approaches. With regard to its spiritual importance, Anavopaya is considered the least important, because it is the most difficult, in which reliance is more upon self-effort than the grace of Shiva or Shakti. We may say, although not definitively, that Anavopaya is the last resort when a yogi fails to attain perfection in Shambhavopaya and Shaktopaya.

3-1 ātmā cittam
Atma is chitta.

Shāmbhavopaya begins with the sutra that atma, the Self, is pure consciousness (chaitanyam). Anavopaya begins with the statement that atma is chitta, the mind. Although they seem to be contradictory, they are not. Here, chitta is a reference to a bound soul's (pasu) natural state of consciousness, which is subject to the triple impurities of egoism, attachments, and delusion. Consciousness is pure when it is free from them and impure when it is subject to them. In both Shambhavopaya and Anavopaya the aim is to progress from the impure to the pure because it is in the purity of consciousness only one attains sameness with Shiva. The Self of an enlightened yogi is chaitanya chitta, awakened, pure consciousness. The Self of a bound jiva is also pure consciousness. However, it is enveloped by impure and unstable consciousness (chapala-chitta), which creates in him the delusion of egoism, individuality, limitation, and separation (anavatva).

Although chitta is loosely translated as the mind, it is more than the mind and consists of both pure and impure consciousness. The impure chitta is made up of the memorial mind (manas), the thinking and discerning mind (buddhi), the autonomous primitive mind, and the self-preservative, egoistic mind (aham), which are filled with predominant desires, thoughts, memories, perceptions, feelings, emotions, images, attachments, latent impressions, etc. The self-illuminated (chaitanya) pure chitta remains hidden in them and is not immediately discernible. For an initiate who is on the path of liberation, this impure mass of consciousness is a minefield and a major source of problems, modifications (vrittis), and afflictions. When the Self is enveloped by ignorance and impurities, one settles with the delusional belief that the mind, the body, and the ego consciousness represent the true Self. The purpose of Anavopaya is to remove this delusion. Hence, this section rightly begins with a reference to chitta because it is where a yogi has to concentrate his effort (Anavopaya) to overcome his animal nature.

3-2 jñānam bandhah

Knowledge (arising from the impure chitta) is binding.

From a spiritual perspective, worldly knowledge is not a blessing but a problem because it is filled with the light or, rather, the darkness of Maya. The knowledge of the world that arises from the impure chitta is also impure because it is filled with ignorance, due to which jivas experience divisions, dualities, and modifications (vrittis) such as pleasure and pain, delusion, confusion, etc. Filed with such impurities and relative knowledge of the objective world, the polluted chitta (surface consciousness) envelops the pure chitta and draws the jivas into the illusory world (samsara māya), keeping them wandering from one birth to another. Thus, although from a worldly perspective, material knowledge has great significance in the survival and continuity of jivas, from a spiritual perspective, it is a problem. It binds the jivas to the mortal world and keeps them oblivious to their true nature. Due to its influence, they remain ignorant of not only their inherent, independent, indivisible, and indestructible, pure consciousness (sahaja chitta) but also their pure Shaktis, which, illuminated by pure consciousness, give them unlimited and indomitable powers and potencies to act like Shiva himself. The bondage of jivas (beings) to samsara is the play of Shiva only. He uses Māya Shaktis to subject them to dualities, desires, and divisions to remain hidden from them and ensure their continuation in the mortal world. Due to ignorance, delusion, and the duality of the knower and the known, beings remain stuck in the jagrat, svapna, and susupta states and do not experience pratyabhijna (the recognition of the truth) or the blissful and self-existent turya. Instead of experiencing the pure consciousness of Shiva (shivatvam), which is natural to us, they experience fragmented consciousness and egoism (anavatvam).

3-3 kalādīnām tattvānām aviveko māyā

Ignorance of tattvas, such as kala, etc., is māya.

The tattvas, such as kala, etc., (kala adi), are a finite set of basic, archetypal organs, parts, ideations, modular structures, or conceptual realities of Shakti (Prakriti) with which she creates the parts and gross bodies of all objects and beings. The Samkhya school identifies 23 of them. Shaiva schools identify 36, namely Shiva, Shakti, Kaala, Niyati, Vidya, Raga, Kala, Sadashiva, Isvara, Shuddha-vidya, Maya, Purusha, Buddhi, Ahamkara, Manas, Prakriti, 15 senses and five elements. The 36 tattvas are classified into three groups, namely kanchuka (divine body), puryastaka (subtle body), and sthuladeha (gross body) in the order in which they envelop the soul from the inside. The tattvas are impure and limited in power because they are controlled by māya. They are illuminated by Shiva (the Self) since they lack illumination of their own. The world is filled with Māya Shaktis and controlled by māya because it is made up of these Maya tattvas only. They manifest in Creation or the Field of Nature as names and forms in Shiva's unending play. By enveloping the Self in three distinct layers, they create the delusion of egoism or the false notion that the mind and body constitute one's true self or identity, and the tattvas are indistinct and integral to oneself, although they are distinct and external. From that false identification also arises the belief of separation (prthkatvata) or the conviction that one is separate and distinct from others or Shiva. In turn, it causes ignorance, worldliness, attraction (raga) and aversion (dvesha), desires, attachments, bondage, and suffering.

3-4 śarīre samhārah kalānām
In the body, destroying kala, etc.

The body is a major obstacle to achieving liberation because it is the seat of Maya and the reason for the limitation of Shaktis and separation from Shiva. However, liberation is not attained by its death or destruction because the body is not the ultimate cause of bondage. The ultimate causes are desires and other impurities of the body and karma. Unless they are resolved, one is not free. Without resolving them, if anyone destroys the body, it is considered a mortal sin and leads to further karma, bondage, and suffering. Therefore, the destruction of the body (sarira samhara) should not be literally interpreted as self-sacrifice. It means that one should dissolve the ego and the beingness (anava) that arise from the tattvas by purifying them. For that, in Anavopaya, a yogi is advised to meditate on all the tattvas, starting from the subtle ones in his innermost body, and to dissolve each of them in his outer gross body. In the final stages, he has to dissolve his connection with the gross body by establishing himself in pure consciousness or in oneness with Shiva, whereby although he lives in his body as a liberated soul (jivanmukta) he loses body awareness and lives as if he does not exist at all as a separate being. The practice also frees him from the influence of the tattvas and their associated impurities, namely egoism, attachments, and delusion. In some schools of Shaivism, the practice of Anavopaya (the dissolution of the limited self) is prescribed as a first step to purify the Shaktis in the body and prepare the initiates for the practice of Shaktopaya. Since, by definition, sariram means any object which is made up of the tattvas of Nature, a yogi may extend this practice to material objects to overcome his attraction and aversion for them.

3-5 nādī samhāra bhūtajaya bhūtakaivalya bhūtaprithaktvāni

By stopping the nadis, conquest of elements, dissolution of elements and separation of elements.

This sutra refers to four types of yogic practices that play an important role in self-purification and the removal of body-related obstacles caused by the impurities of māya. Nadi samhara refers to the practice of removing blockages in the main nadies (Ida, Sushma, and Pingala), which prevent the free flow of prana in the nadis and Kundalini between the Chakras. It also refers to the practice of breath control (pranayama) and of arresting the breath (kumbhaka) externally (bahya) in the nostrils (bahya kumbhaka) and internally(antar) in the breath passages such as prana, apana, udana, etc. Both practices lead to the purification of the mind and body through the triple transformations of bhuta jaya, bhuta kaivalya, and bhuta prithaktva. Bhuta jaya means the conquest of desires and passions in the body, such as thirst, hunger and sexual desires which arise from the elements. Bhuta kaivalya means the dissolution of physical and mental afflictions such as disease, aging, sickness, etc., which are caused by the elements. Bhuta prithaktva means the ability to distinguish and separate the Self from the gross and subtle bodies and move freely, if necessary, without them. These abilities naturally arise in yogis without any practice or preparation when, by the grace of the guru or Shiva, they attain innate knowing (sahaja vidya) through oneness with the Self and dissolution in the all-knowing pure consciousness. In a broader and philosophical sense, conquering the elements means mastering the elements and the desires and afflictions that arise from them due to attraction, aversion, and repeated association. Dissolving the elements means dissolving the identity and attachment that are caused by them, and separating the elements means detaching oneself from the elemental body and remaining stabilized in the pure chitta. They are achieved through the conquest of the mind and body and establishing oneself in the Self with oneness.

3-6 mohāvaranāt siddhih

Siddhi, while still being veiled by moha.

Moha means delusion or the power of māya. A yogi may gain supernatural powers (siddhis) with nadi samhara, bhuta jaya, bhuta kaivalya, bhuta prithaktva, etc., while still being veiled by māya Shaktis. When it happens without corresponding purification and removal of obstacles, he may attain limited powers (mita siddhi) but not the pure tattva (Shiva) or supreme siddhi (self-realization). Whatever supernatural powers or siddhis he gains will remain veiled and limited by delusion, whereby he may possess some powers but will not enter the realm of the luminous Self or experience bliss. With inferior siddhis, he may enjoy the pleasures of māya tattvas and the elemental body but not the bliss of the supreme Self (para tattva). By that, he may even become distracted and fall. The essence of this is that yogis must focus on self-purification to attain liberation but not become distracted in the middle. They should be aware of the play of māya since she continues to be active until perfection is achieved. Therefore, they should remain on guard and solely focus on self-purification through a strict code of conduct and spiritual practice, illuminating their minds with the thoughts of Shiva and purifying the tattvas, nadis, and chakras in their bodies through mudras, breathing, khechari, etc., while keeping the Māya Shaktis under control with the help of Iccha, Kriya and Jnana Shaktis. Purifying their gross and subtle bodies through them and overcoming impurities and desired-ridden actions, they must awaken the self-existing illumination in them. If a yogi persists in such efforts, he experiences spanda, the pulsation of the supreme consciousness, or the dance of Shiva himself. By that union or oneness in the state of non-duality, he realizes that he is the supreme Shiva and experiences the supreme Siddhi.

3-7 mohajayād anantābhogāt sahajavidyājayah

With the unquestionable conquest of māya, the triumph of sahajavidya.

The key to success in Anavopaya is the unquestionable conquest of Maya or the delusion that the body is the Self. It is achieved by overcoming the triple impurities of egoism, desires, and delusion. As can be seen, Anavopaya focuses on the impurities of the mind and body, viewing the body as a battleground of Maya Shaktis and a major obstacle to attaining oneness with Shiva. The Shaktis are not evil. They play their parts, performing their duties and fulfilling their obligation to the Supreme Lord as ordained. The lower Shaktis work against the yogi's cherished goals while the higher Shaktis assist him to the extent they can to purify himself and attain perfection. Overcoming moha and māya is required to enter the supreme state of Shiva and attain pure knowledge, also known as natural or inborn knowledge (sahaja vidya). As the supreme reality (parama tattva), Shiva is the eternally pure Self (shuddha tattva), in contrast to the Shakti tattvas, which are impure in the beings when they are separated from him and mixed up with the gunas, but pure when they are illuminated by him and united with him. There is no place for any impurity in Shiva.

Therefore, when the Shaktis join him, they become filled with his purity and luminosity and return to their natural (sahaja) and harmonious state. Sahaja vidya means knowledge (vidya) that is natural or innate (sahaja) to the Self. It is the highest knowledge that exists only in Shiva or the Self and cannot be accessed by any means other than entering oneness or becoming absorbed in him without duality. In short, it is the all-pervading and all-knowing absolute state of Shiva. There is nothing beyond it. It is independent, self-existent, established in the eternal dharma, and arises when the bondage (samsara) is destroyed and when delusion (moha) is overcome, whereby the omniscient knowledge of the supreme Self (sahaja vidya) becomes self-evident. Moha jaya, or victory over delusion, may arise through intense yoga practice (shaktopaya) or through the annihilation of the ego and the limited Mayas (anavopaya). It may also automatically arise in a Shiva yogi when he attains perfection in self-purification or earns the grace of Shiva (Shambhavopaya). With that, his delusion is destroyed in endless ways for the endless bliss (anantabhogat). Since delusion manifests in various ways, the victory over it must always be complete and perfect. This is one of the benefits of Anavopaya.

3-8 jāgrad dvitīyakarah

Jagrat becomes secondary.

Kara means a hand or a beam of light. Jagrat means the wakeful world or the wakeful state. For a yogi who has attained oneness with Shiva and is firmly established in the original knowledge (sahaja vidya), he becomes the first, and the wakeful world he sees within himself becomes the second, as he sees himself as the Self of all, and the objective world as his emanation (kara), projection or extension within his own consciousness. In the innate knowing of the Self, the wakeful world appears to a sahaja yogi as illuminated by his own effulgence, just as he sees the sun illuminating the worlds and bringing them to life. He innately knows himself as the seer, the knower, the subject, the first, the Self (aham atma) and the supreme Self (aham brahmasmi), and sees the world as the known, the object, the second, not this (neti), all this (idam sarvam), or the not-self (anatma). This is the non-dualistic experience of Shiva's absolute and supreme reality, which arises from the yogi's oneness with him. At the same time, he knows that the world is a part of himself, caused and illuminated by him and filled with his Shaktis and pure consciousness. Since the Self is indivisible, the reality which arises from it is also indivisible. Those who are established in it do not perceive the world as separate or distinct or second but as themselves. For the Shiva yogis, consciousness is everything. It is the first and the only reality. They do not discard any of it, just the impurities that cloud it and prevent them from knowing themselves without duality and delusion.

3-9 nartaka ātmā

The Self is the Dance Master.

An ignorant devotee in a state of duality and delusion perceives the world as Shiva's dance drama and everyone in it, including himself as a player or actor, enacting different roles. Because of anava (egoism), he cannot help seeing the world with duality, as if he is distinct from it and from Shiva, in spite of the knowledge or understanding to the contrary he might have gained from studying the scriptures or hearing from the masters. A self-realized yogi who is firmly established in the pure and undifferentiated consciousness of Shiva sees it differently. For him, everything is Shiva. In the state of non-duality, he sees himself as the dance master as well as the actor who plays diverse roles in diverse forms for his own enjoyment on a stage set by himself, within himself, and for himself. Since he is free from the duality of subject and object or the knower and the known, he also sees himself as Shiva only, envisioning oneness in wakeful, dream, and deep sleep states and performing the five functions of creation, preservation, dissolution, suppression, and expression in his own creation. He enters this state of oneness or nonduality through direct experience when he is established in Shiva without an identity or individuality of his own. With the pure knowledge (sahaja vidya) and omniscience which arise from that experience of unity and oneness, he becomes innately aware that all this here is his play only, in which he is the actor (nartaka atma) as well as the spectator (sakshi), enacting and witnessing his own drama. Remaining awake when everyone is asleep, he sees the world not only as his projection but also as his playground. With the dissolution of his egoism and delusion, he is no more subject to vikalpa (distinction or duality). All that is becomes his own projection, his dream.

3-10 rango'ntarātmā
The stage is the inner Self.

For a self-realized yogi who is absorbed in Shiva, the Self in him (antaratma) or the consciousness in him is the stage. It does not mean that he sees the outside world any differently. Anything that appears in his consciousness or arises from it is a part of his creation. Antaratma, in this context, means the pure consciousness of Shiva or the inner Self, which is also the Self of all, not the individual Self (purusha) of the Samkhyas. When a yogi transcends duality and attains Shiva, he sees the world as existing in him only. What appears to others as external and distinct from them appears to him as internal and indistinct (savikalpa). In other words, his oneness (samadhi) or the transcendental state of turya continues even in his wakeful state, dream, and deep sleep states. His consciousness, which is now pure and identical to that of Shiva and filled with uninterrupted awareness, continues in all states undisturbed and undivided, even when his surface mind is subject to interruptions and modifications and outwardly, he may seem to be engaged in actions and conversations. The truth that the world is both a subject and an object is never lost to him. It is an object when viewed from a limited perspective with limited and bound consciousness, but an emanation or a self-projection when one is firmly established in nonduality and absorbed in Shiva consciousness (shiva bhava). In that vision of Shiva, the yogi sees everything as his own play and himself playing multiple roles in different guises as the enjoyer and the enjoyed or the subject and object. Yet, he remains untouched as he does not become involved, and even if he does, his oneness with Shiva neutralizes all the consequences. Having become the Self of all, he witnesses everything as internal to him. It is not the same with ordinary people who see the world with duality. They view the external world as a stage set by God for their enjoyment. Thereby, they engage in desire-ridden actions as if they have a divine right to enjoy this world and remain bound.

3-11 prekśakānīndriyāni

The sense organs are the spectators.

Be it a human being, an animal, a bird, a worm, or an insect, the senses are always the spectators who connect their internal organs with the external world. Without the senses, nothing can be seen or enjoyed. Even the embodied Self, we have to admit, witnesses the drama of existence through the senses only. The jiva's experiences and memorial knowledge arise primarily from the senses. This is true whether it is an enlightened yogi, an ordinary human being, or a primate. However, the mode, orientation, or propensity (pravritti) in them differs. In ignorant humans and other jivas (pasus), the senses are always outbound. Although they may be resting, inactive, or in deep sleep, their senses remain mostly active and in the outward mode only. Because of delusion, they perceive that the world is external to them, their minds and senses are internal, and they are interacting with the world through their senses. Their intelligence also does not help them see the unity underlying the diversity they witness through their senses. They can see only their isolated consciousness in action but not the universal consciousness that pervades all and exists in all. Hence, they cannot perceive the truth that all that exists outside arises from the same consciousness that perceives them. This is not the case with the awakened Shiva yogis. Having been purified and illuminated by the brilliance of pure intelligence (dhi), their senses are propelled by pure Shaktis and illuminated intelligence rather than māya Shaktis and delusion. Their illuminated pure consciousness perceives what their senses cannot. Hence, they perceive the truth of things in oneness from the inside as well as from the outside. With their senses withdrawn and turned inward and blissfully absorbed in themselves, they become spectators to the drama that unfolds within themselves and outside on the stage of the infinite, pure consciousness, which is now their natural (sahaja) state, without duality, division, or distinction.

3-12 *dhīvaśāt sattvasiddhih*

By controlling dhi, purity is attained.

In Anavopaya, purity is the key to success. It is attained by the predominance of sattva through yoga and by absorption in pure consciousness upon liberation. In both cases, controlling the dhi (buddhi) or intelligence is important. Dhi refers to the mental brilliance which gives us the ability to think, analyze, discern truth from falsehood, and overcome delusion. It is the higher faculty of the mind and the highest tattva of Nature and plays an important role in controlling the senses and suppressing the modes (gunas). Purity (sattva) is a precondition in all the three paths to Shiva. Only the purest of the pure earn the right to enter his realm and experience oneness with his universal consciousness, which is infinite and filled with the purity and effulgence of countless suns. Buddhi (the organ of intellect) is the seat of dhi and the highest of all the tattvas in the subtle (puryastaka) and gross (sthula) bodies. It is also the seat of pure Shaktis where the illumination of the Self shines. In the deluded states, all 36 tattvas, including buddhi, are under the control of māya Shaktis. Without freeing them from their control, it is difficult to attain sattva siddhi and progress on the path. Invoking the pure Shaktis of buddhi and cultivating discernment and righteous conduct, a yogi purifies his tattvas and attains sattva siddhi. The touch of Shiva is purifying in itself, in which case control over intelligence is easily attained. When pure knowledge (sahaja vidya) arises in a yogi by any means, his mind and body are instantly purified, and his consciousness shines with the effulgence of Shiva. In that state, with innate knowing naturally arising, yogis gain effortless insight into the nature of the tattvas and the ability to control them and purify them at will in others also. It means that they can purify others and prepare them for liberation by their touch or will.

3-13 siddhah svatantrabhāvah
The state of freedom is attained.

By controlling dhi and merging with Shiva, the state of freedom is attained in which knowledge spontaneously arises, and one has the freedom to exercise his free will and act independently. True freedom is the ability to exercise free will and act freely with knowledge and mastery without restraints, limitations, or conditions. It is the state of the Self, which is always free. It is true even when it is embodied and bound to samsara. The Self exists in its own dimension, untouched by materiality and the impurities of samsara. Even the kanchuka, the innermost body, has no access to it although its radiance may be reflected by it. It cannot be known by any means other than by becoming one with it. When a yogi is fully absorbed in it without duality and delusion, he also becomes free. His svantatrabhava (state of freedom) arises from his union with Shiva (the Self) and detachment and independence from his mind and body. When he gains insight into the nature of the tattvas with pure discernment (dhi) and unites with Shiva's pure consciousness (sahaja vidya), he also gains freedom from the controlling and deluding Shaktis. Instead of being a slave (dasa) to them, which is the norm in the jivas, he becomes their lord (pati) with irresistible will. With the control thus gained over Iccha, Jnana and Kriya Shaktis, unlimited potencies and powers naturally manifest in him, with which he develops the power to control not only the tattvas and Shaktis in him but also his breath, mind, senses, etc. Many supernatural powers also manifest in him simultaneously, including the ability to use the mantras (mantra virya) and will to control the elements (bhutajaya), the world (vishva vasikarana), the tattvas in others' bodies and objects in the world.

3-14.1 yathā tatra tathānyatra

As there, so elsewhere.

As in the body, so elsewhere, a yogi enjoys unobstructed, unrestrained freedom. Final liberation means absolute freedom from every want, desire, attachment, and limitation that conditions human life and actions. It results in unlimited potency and willpower to do anything, be anything, or achieve anything without attracting consequences to oneself or one's independence. The Self exists by itself without associations, obligations, and dependencies, which means that it does not depend upon any other entity or power to know, act, use its will, or achieve any end. That freedom or independence arises naturally in those who are established in Shiva with oneness and partake in his natural state. They are independent not only within their minds and bodies but also outside, where their consciousness and Shaktis flow and illuminate. They extend their reach into the world with their minds and intelligence (dhi) beyond where their senses could go. In the unified state, which may arise from the practice of Shāmbhavopaya or Shaktopaya or Anavopaya, they gain control not only over their limited selves but also the whole world. Their freedom is not limited to any place, time, measure, condition, or circumstance but extends to wherever their attention goes. As the lords of the Shaktis, they potentially possess unlimited powers to know, grasp, create, dissolve, conceal, reveal, and uphold. Just as they are independent in their bodies with the ability to control Iccha, Jnana, and Kriya Shaktis, so do they remain elsewhere also. As Shiva himself, the yogi who attains oneness with him remains free and self-willed in worldly life and spiritual life, and in wakeful, dream, and deep sleep states.

3-14.2 *visargasvābhāvyād abahih sthitestatsthitih*

What has spread out is not external but internally located.

The duality or the division of external and internal arises in ignorant people but not in the awakened ones. For a self-realized yogi, what has spread out or exists outside as his body, the world, or the world body is not external to him but internal only. It exists from him as an aspect of him or an extension of him or his consciousness. For him, everything is filled with I-am-ness or with Shiva (shivamayam) in a purely subjective state of self-existence without any otherness. He does not perceive anything as external to him because his consciousness extends in all directions without a second. Everything arises and subsides in him only. The world becomes his play on the stage of his consciousness. The same consciousness, filled with radiant Shaktis, extends from him and pervades as well as envelops all the worlds, objects, and beings. Since there is nothing external to him, all reality manifests in him in his subjective, unified state as himself. Although what arises from him as his creation (visarga) is not the same as his pure Self, it is but a part of his universal body, illuminated by him. The objective reality is perceived by the senses as other than oneself. The known is external to the knower. Hence, it is the not-self. This distinction does not arise in a self-illumined Shiva yogi, who perceives it as a part of his extended consciousness. Hence, what is seen as external by the mind and senses is seen by the yogi's intelligence (dhi) as a part of himself and internal to him.

Notes: This particular sutra is not found in many classical commentaries and transcripts. We found it in a Hindi commentary by B. N. Pandit, and thought it would be appropriate to include it here since it has a correlation to the previous one and extends its thought process. To preserve the original order, we listed it as 14.2.

3-15 bījāvadhānam

Concentration on the seed.

Concentration on the seed means one should practice concentration on the Self (shuddha tattva), who is the source (seed) of all, or concentration on the Shaktis hidden in the seed mantras (bijaksharas), or concentration on the prana Shakti flowing in the body. All three approaches are useful and helpful to cultivate sattva siddhi and become established in the innate state of pure knowing (sahaja vidya). A yogi who practices Anavopaya is never diverted or separated from Shiva. Whether he is engaged in contemplative inquiry or worldly activity and whether his senses are outbound or inbound, his attention is always fixed upon Shiva, who is the source and support of all knowledge, awareness, activity, and self-will. The object of concentration may be Shiva or Shakti, a point of light, flame, a mystic symbol, or a bija (seed) mantra. Whatever it may be, he remains one-pointed and fixed on the object of concentration, with his consciousness illuminated by the triple Shaktis and filled with the awareness of Shiva and his mind absorbed in itself between thoughts and movements. The mind of a deluded person is drawn out and scatted among the sense objects. He may occasionally remember Shiva, but not always. Therefore, his potencies and consciousness remain limited and mixed up with light and darkness. The self-Illumined yogi keeps alive his connection with Shiva. His awareness is never diverted from him, even when his mind wanders or senses are active. He fuels his Shaktis through concentration, meditation, chanting of mantras and other means so that he remains so absorbed in the consciousness of Shiva that he sees everything as Shiva (himself) in a state of nonduality. He sees himself in everything and as the cause and effect. Even if his perceptions arise from his sense organs, he sees them as the numerous manifestations or forms of Shiva, filled with his illumination and Shaktis. This state arises naturally when a yogi attains oneness with Shiva and becomes dissolved in pure consciousness. The consciousness that ordinarily dogs our minds ceases to be a problem in him and submits to his will unconditionally. Such is the power of the yogi who has merged his consciousness with that of Shiva.

3-16 āsanasthah sukham hrade nimajjati

Abiding in asana, effortlessly sinks into the lake.

Asanastha literally means sitting down in a particular posture with firm control. In this context, it may also mean to hold oneself firmly in a fixed state with the mind fixed and absorbed in the awareness of Shiva without distractions and duality. To practice any asana for a long time, one requires a strong will to control the agitating Shaktis and hold the mind and body steady. This sutra suggests that by controlling the body with the help of Shaktis and fixing the mind constantly upon Shiva with one-pointedness (ekagrata), one can quickly sink into the lake of pure consciousness without having to practice the rather painful and tortuous austerities and the difficult techniques of pratyahara, pranayama, dharana, dhyana, etc. When one is in control and harmony, with the Shaktis in the body, progress becomes easier, and one can effortlessly sink into the infinite ocean of blissful consciousness and become dissolved in it. The paths to Shiva are many. Some of them are long and arduous, and some are easier. This sutra mentions the easier one, where a yogi takes refuge in the triple Shaktis and seeks their intervention to purify himself. When he does that, the Shaktis carry him across the ocean of samsara to the other side. He does not have to torture his body or subject himself to painful austerities. He has to draw his mind to Shiva and keep remembering him continuously even in between two thoughts and movements. If he keeps saturating his mind with the uninterrupted awareness of Shiva, the goddesses will become his companions and protectors and save him from the poison of suffering that arises in him due to the resistance of Maya or the natural modifications of the mind and body. This is one of the secrets of tantra, which is cryptically mentioned here. Once you fill your mind with Shiva and invite Para Shakti into your body, who represents the purest and the brightest Shaktis in the universe, and surrender to her, she will take control of your being and purify it so that you do not have to practice dharana or dhyana, etc., or follow any other technique. Instead, you have to remain passive, absorbed in the thoughts of Shiva, allowing the Shaktis to transform you and prepare you for the awakening. This sutra may have other meanings in the left-hand practices of esoteric tantras, which the scope of this work does not allow to elaborate.

3-17 *svamātrā nirmānam āpādayati*

With his Shakti, he manifests creation.

There can be no creation outside Shiva. Everything has to arise from him and within him only. The Shaktis are a part of him, although, for the sake of upholding creation, they may manifest duality in the jivas and create the illusion of their separation and distinction from him. Just like Shiva, the Mother Goddess, Parashakti is also infinite. Since creation cannot contain them, each of them participates in it in their limited aspects. The same holds for all the beings who manifest in creation. They contain the essence of Shiva and Shakti but not their true dimensions or full potencies. Even in oneness, it is doubtful whether any yogi or emanation will ever attain the full potencies of Shiva or Shakti or truly match them in their universal aspects. The Upanishads affirm this, stating that Brahman is without a second (advitiyam). The world arises from Parashakti by the will of Shiva, in which several of her manifestations (Shaktis) participate, which are pure, impure, or mixed. As an inseparable part of Shiva (the self), she infuses her creations with knowledge, liveliness (chaitanya), and consciousness (chidrasa). Thus, Shiva is the essential cause, and Matrka is the material cause. Without them acting in unison, there is no creation, forms, duality, or beingness. With the absorption in Shiva consciousness (sahaja vidya), which arises from oneness with Shiva as a result of uninterrupted awareness of him, a yogi realizes his inseparable connection with Parashakti in the nondual state of Shiva. He innately knows that with her immense powers, which are now his (sva matra), he can manifest reality and illuminate it with the knowledge and power of himself. In the state of nonduality, indistinguishably united with Shakti, he sees the world as his own play and himself as its cause and support. With the innate knowledge and power that arise from him thus, he can potentially manifest anything by his mere will.

3-18 vidyā avināśe janma vināśah

With the indestructible knowledge, the end of birth.

Rebirth is not because the jivas need to be rescued; it is because the Self has to be liberated from the control of the Shaktis and returned to its absolute state of freedom. It is a game between Shiva and Shakti, and the jivas are instrumental in its continuation. The jivas should not be considered victims in this game since they are but their forms only. The jivas have the option to escape from it, but to utilize it they have to attain human birth and acquire the right knowledge and awareness, which, in this case, the knowledge and awareness of Shiva and Shakti. True knowledge (vidya) destroys the causes of birth and death and, thereby, bondage. Liberation means the end of birth and death, which is the state of immortality. The cause of samsara is ignorance and delusion. The cause of liberation is true knowledge or pure knowledge, which is revealed only to the knower of the Self, the true Siddha. The knowledge which arises from the mind and senses is destructible, mutable, and impure, and the cause of karma, suffering, and bondage. It is destructible and mutable because it is subject to modifications, gain, and loss. It may help you in worldly life, but it is an obstacle to liberation. Since it arises from ignorance and delusion, it is also unreliable as a measure of truth or to ascertain truth. It is destroyed when the indestructible knowledge of the Self arises in the innate self-knowing, which is pure consciousness filled with the brilliance and awareness of Shiva and Shakti in their unified and absolute state as One. It is indestructible because it arises from the indestructible Self. It is also pure and original because it is beyond the reach of the impure tattvas and Shaktis. Hence, it is also known as pure knowledge (suddha vidya), which arises naturally (sahaja) when the darkness of the chitta is removed, just as the sun appears when the clouds are blown away. The self-knowing state of a yogi is independent, original, infinite, indivisible, and blissful. When it manifests, all traces of ignorance and other impurities such as egoism, attachment, and delusion are destroyed, and one is permanently released from the cycle of births and deaths. Those who enter the abode of Shiva through it and partake in his essential nature (Shiva bhava) never return to the mortal world to take another birth in any womb.

3-19 kavargādisu māheśvaryādyāh paśumātarah

Mahesvari and others of the "ka" group of Shaktis are mothers of pashus.

In the beginning of creation, Parashakti divides herself into numerous forms and becomes the mother of numerous ignorant beings who possess animal nature from birth. All the jivas who are born thus are known as pashus. They are limited beings filled with ignorance (about themselves and Shiva) and subject to the triple impurities of egoism (anava), attachments (pasas), and delusion (moha). These impurities keep them under the control of Māya-Shaktis or pashu-shaktis, who belong to the Matrka-chakra or the force matrix of Shakti, the Universal Mother. As explained before, all the sounds in the Sanskrit alphabet, from "a" to "ksha," (अ to क्ष) are represented by various goddesses, who combine within themselves the triple powers of will (Iccha), knowledge (jnana) and action (kriya). Through their permutations and combinations and by joining with objects, these mothers create a diversity of names and forms. The Shaktis belong to two primary groups known as Bija and Yoni. The goddesses of the Bija class represent vowel sounds, and those of Yoni represent the sounds of letters from "ka" to "ksha." As their name implies, the Yoni class of goddesses are mothers of all those who are born in the womb of Nature, which means practically everyone. They are also known as Māya Shaktis because they veil the embodied souls (jivātma) with ignorance and keep them bound and deluded. A yogi should be aware that the pashu-matas do not easily grant liberation because they do not like to undo themselves or become irrelevant. They remain active in the body, even after one has realized the true nature of the tattva and attained the pure knowledge of the Self (suddha vidya). Therefore, yogis who want to attain Shiva tattva should remain on guard, knowing that the Māya Shaktis may still try to trick them and cause their downfall. How they should overcome this problem is explained in the next sutra.

3-20 trisu caturtham tailavadāsecyam

Into the three should be dropped the fourth like oil.

The fourth is Turya. The three are Jagrat, Svapna and Susupti. They are the states of consciousness. It may be recalled that the seventh sutra in the Shambhavopaya section, which we already discussed, affirms that by engaging the mind constantly in the uninterrupted and exclusive awareness of Shiva, a yogi can bring the blissful state of turya into the other three states of wakefulness, dream, and deep sleep states. In the eleventh sutra of the same section, we are introduced to the idea that as the lord of the senses (viresa), an enlightened yogi becomes the enjoyer of turya (turyabhokta) in the other three states also as his consciousness remains illuminated by the constant awareness of Shiva. These assertions lead to the conclusion that a yogi should not be content with the momentary experiences of turya or absorption in the blissful state of Shiva. He should try to prolong and extend such experience to the other three states and make it as frequent as possible until turya keeps flowing into his consciousness constantly and becomes his natural state. If it does not happen frequently, he should at least keep remembering it and keep his mind open to its possibility. Once it becomes regular, his consciousness becomes elevated, illuminated, and firmly established in the blissful state of pure consciousness, and he attains oneness with Shiva. Thus, this sutra suggests that transcendental experiences should not have to be otherworldly. Through effort, they can be brought into the realm of conscious experience and everyday reality. By constantly bringing the bliss of turya into the other three states and illuminating them, a yogi can constantly and consciously experience oneness with Shiva and remain immersed in a blissful state. By that, he can also foil the attempts by the veiling mothers to trap him or disturb him.

3-21 magnah svacittena praviset

Becoming absorbed, let him enter through his own consciousness.

Through mental absorption (chitta magna), by abiding in the steady state of contemplation (asana), the yogi should reach the Self through his own consciousness (svachitta). According to Mrityjidbhattaraka, it is a better alternative to the standard practices of pranayama, dharana, dhyana, etc. By that, he can overcome his dependence upon his mind and body and his attachment to them. The mind (chitta) is the cause as well as the means to remove the impurities of egoism, ignorance, and delusion, which are fueled by the veiling influence of the Māya Shaktis of the "ka" group. When you know the cause, why should you go around it? Attack it directly at the root and remove it. Therefore, the best way to remove the impurities of the limited self (pashu) is to attack their causes, which remain hidden in the chitta itself. When a yogi withdraws his mind (chitta) from shining material objects of the external world and engages it through bhairavi mudra in the contemplative inquiry of the matrkas of the "ka" group, he awakens them in himself, just as fire awakens the sleeping coal. By soaking the wakeful, dream, and sleep states with the consciousness of turya, he successfully removes from his limited self the impurities of egoism, ignorance, and delusion in all four states and remains established in the blissful and infinite supreme consciousness of Shiva. Its sustained practice weakens the memorial mind (manas), animal vitality (chetana), veiling powers (Māya Shaktis), and the ego (jivātma). As the body becomes pure and radiant with the power of Bhairava (absolute reality), the limited mind (chitta) is dissolved, and the limited being (pashu) is released from the cycle of births and deaths.

3-22 prāna samācāre samadarśanam

With the slow movement of prana arises the seeing of sameness.

Sameness means being equal to pairs of opposites, such as heat and cold. It arises due to the absence of desires or subduing of desires when the yogi is free from attraction and aversion. The Bhagavadgita defines it as yoga (the highest state) itself and prescribes detachment and renunciation to cultivate it. Sameness is oneness only since the feeling of differentiation or distinct (prthak bhavana) also disappears with it. Here, breath control or slowing of the prana is mentioned. Slow and steady breathing is useful if you want to control your emotions and restlessness and experience equanimity. In adept yogis, who are free and detached, it becomes their natural state. When a yogi realizes that nonduality is the only self-existent reality and that the same Self exists in everyone, he settles with sameness, seeing the same reality everywhere and in everything. In that state, his gaze becomes steady and his breath slow. In the pure state of oneness, when his mind and body are illuminated by pure consciousness, his prana flows slowly as it carries more energy and vitality due to the presence of pure Shaktis. Further, as he is not easily agitated, he can sustain himself even with a minimal supply of prana. Samachara literally means slow, measured, balanced, steady, or equal movement. Samadarshana means equanimity or sameness. It is the seeing of everything with an equal eye, without duality or distinction. It may arise when one transcends attraction and aversion by conquering the mind and body or when one becomes firmly established in the consciousness of Shiva and sees oneself everywhere in numerous bodies and objects in different guises as one's own play. It may also arise through contemplative introspection (chitta nimagna) when the limited consciousness of the mind is purified and becomes utterly tranquil, without vrittis, and yields to pure consciousness. When that supreme state becomes natural and common to all the four states, breathing becomes subtle, smooth, and steady, as if one is not breathing at all. A yogi may temporarily induce it through slow breathing and settle in sameness through sustained practice. Having been firmly established in pure consciousness, sameness, and non-duality and seeing the flow of prana everywhere, he may also absorb prana in various other ways without having to breathe at all.

3-23 madhye'vara prasarah

In the middle, avara prasarah.

The loss of momentum, which arises due to duality and divisions in the middle of turya or nirvikalpa samadhi, is known as avara prasara. In some renditions, it is mentioned as avara prasavah. Whatever the terminology is, this sutra suggests that the intensity of the turya experience or Shiva consciousness may weaken. It may happen for any number of reasons, due to distractions, loss of attention and willpower, interruptions and disturbances during samadhi, or the unpredictable nature of turya itself. It can happen to anyone if they are inattentive, take their practice for granted, or do not exercise proper control during the chanting of mantras and bijaksharas or when engaged in mudras, meditation, concentration, withdrawal of the senses, pranayama, etc. In Anavopaya, due to the difficulty of the path itself, yogis' resolve and motivation may remain high in the beginning at the prospect of beginning a new journey as well as at the end at the prospect of reaching the goal. In the middle, they may also be distracted by Maya-Shaktis who rarely give up, resulting in the weakening of their resolve and motivation and failure to maintain continuous one-pointed awareness of Shiva. As a result, the intensity and continuity of their turya experience may decline. Shiva yogis should, therefore, persevere and remain steadfast in their practice, guarding themselves against distractions and disturbances. They should keep the flow of their breath (prana) steady and firm, strengthen their resolve, and not yield to any temptations or shortcuts. How adepts do it is explained in the next sutra.

3-24 mātrāsu svapratyaya sandhāne nastasya punarutthānam

By uniting the Self with the objects and the like, the loss is regained.

The mind tends to become easily distracted and lose focus when engaged in the duality of subject and object. However, when the duality disappears, and the knower or the seer only remains, the mind has nowhere to go and no other distraction. The senses remain inactive and withdrawn since they cannot perceive the seer or the Self for whom they work. A yogi may experience temporary loss of nirvikalpa samadhi (formless self-absorption) or the turya state when he is engaged with the objects in the wakeful and dream states and when a part of his awareness is disconnected from his pure Self, resulting in duality. It may also arise during his sadhana when he is engaged in contemplative introspection (chitta majna), in sameness (sama darshanam), in slow and steady breathing (prana samachara), or the chanting of the matrka varnas. When his connection with the pure, nondual consciousness is lost, duality and division resurface in him in the place of nonduality, and he becomes distracted. This sutra suggests that a yogi can recover from this problem by reconnecting the Self to the objects he perceives and regaining his unified consciousness. In other words, when he sees objects, he should remember that all that he sees is the Self or Shiva and remain focused on that awareness. By remembering that the Self or Shiva is all this and he is present in all, he can regain his transcendental state and reestablish himself in the steady flow of nonduality, sameness, and oneness of turya. He may also do it by focusing on the subtle sound that flows uninterruptedly in the deeper states of his consciousness or upon the sound of his breathing or that of a bijaskhara.

3-25 śivatulyo jāyate

He becomes Shiva-like.

By that constant attention and remembrance and by repeatedly drawing his mind back to the awareness of Shiva or the Self, the yogi can overcome the intermittent dilution of the turya state and keep it steady and strong until it becomes his natural state in all four states. A jivanmukta who attains liberation while in the body is not the same as the liberated Self (mukta) because he still has a connection with his body, which poses its own problems, being a production of Nature and subject to aging, sickness, etc. He becomes a pure Self only when he finally leaves his body, never to return to take another birth. When a yogi reaches the end of turya, having overcome the problems and obstacles along the way in sustaining it, his mind becomes illuminated with Shiva consciousness, and he enters that state which is beyond turya (turyatita). It is the state of the pure Self, which is complete, independent, brilliant, and auspicious, just as Shiva is. In that natural state of blissful consciousness (chidananda), omniscience (sarvajna), and omnipotence (sarvakartutva), he sees himself in all, without distinction, duality or disturbance. At this stage, he is similar to Shiva or Shiva-like (shivatulya) but not Shiva himself because he is still in the embodied state and not fully disengaged from his body. Although he is a tattvajna who has knowledge and power over the tattvas and Shaktis and who can remain indifferent and detached from them, he is still subject to the natural functions and limitations of his body because he obtains the body through prarabda (past) karma and cannot leave it until his time comes.

Upon death, when he finally leaves his body, he merges with Shiva and becomes one with him. Until then, he has to remain in the body.

3-26 śarīravrttirvratam
Penance through bodily functions.

A liberated soul does not engage in bodily functions because of desires or necessity. Although he is liberated from the body and the cycle of births and deaths, he performs them as acts of penance or worship to keep it alive. Penance, in this context, means he practices self-control toward his mind and body. The body plays an important role in our existence as well as liberation. Without the gross, physical body, there is no possibility of liberation. Even gods know it. Although the body is an obstacle in self-transformation and liberation, it is a critical development in the spiritual evolution of life on earth and an important vehicle for those who practice yoga and austerities to overcome their animal nature and impurities. It is also the meeting ground between Shiva and Shakti, where they have an opportunity to reunite and shine with their pure illumination. For the yogis, their bodies serve as their testing grounds where they can control their Māyā Shaktis, gunas, and desires and become their true lords. Its importance is not diminished even after one attains liberation. Those jivanmuktas who attain liberation in their bodies still have a lot of work to do since they are still subject to their prarabdha karma. Although they are free from all obligations, they still need to engage in bodily functions to maintain their bodies and stay alive until their destined time. However, since they are united with Shiva, whatever bodily functions they perform in their pure state, such as bathing, eating, speaking, drinking, breathing, etc., become acts of penance only as they engage in nishkama karma (desireless actions) and perform them with sacrificial attitude. Their penance through such actions continues even when they are asleep because sleep is also a bodily function in which the body becomes an offering in worship to Shiva as Kapalika, the Guardian of Night.

3-27 kathā japah

His speech becomes japa.

The body is the polluter or consciousness. All impurities and desires arise from it. If the body is purified, consciousness becomes pure. Speech becomes pure and divine. Therefore, the speech of a purified soul has the auspicious quality of a japa or sacred muttering. It is pure and illuminated since it arises from pure consciousness, without the intervention of bodily desires and attachments, and is filled with the radiant power of higher Shaktis. Whatever he says radiates the effulgence and power of his pure nature, just as the sacred mantras and sacred syllables. His words possess the transformative power to manifest reality, clear the cloud of delusion, or awaken an ignorant disciple. Therefore, people go to him to seek his company, find inspiration, or receive his blessings, although he may prefer to avoid them. Japa means chanting or muttering of sacred words and sounds. A yogi who is united with Shiva and filled with his effulgent supreme consciousness knows that he is the transcendental Shiva who exists in all and the source of all. Filled with pure consciousness, devoid of the impurities that are natural to the body, he verily becomes Shiva, pure consciousness, endowed with supreme knowledge and power. In him, all Shaktis, now disentangled from their association with the body, become pure and resplendent and participate in the sacrifice of knowledge, radiating his effulgence, knowledge, and wisdom through his speech and actions. Awakened Shiva Yogis are not obliged to perform japa or any action, since they are already liberated and are not required to engage in obligatory duties. However, since they embody pure consciousness and supreme knowledge and intelligence just like Shiva, their speech becomes a sacred utterance, a form of worship (japa) in adoration of the Self, illuminated by the power of pure Shaktis. When breathing, emitting the sound "soham," the yogi performs hamsa japa; when speaking about Shiva, he performs nama japa; when feeling the sensations in his body, he engages in Shakti Japa, and when he is absorbed in the Self, which is Pranava, he performs the uninterrupted, seedless Nishkala Japa.

3-28 dānam ātmajñānam

His teaching of self-knowledge is a gift.

The liberated yogi's teaching of self-knowledge is a sacred gift to the initiates. It is a gift or act of charity because he imparts that sacred knowledge without desires and expectations as a sacrifice for a righteous cause. We may say he does it to serve Shiva, but it cannot be since he is free from delusion and duality and has become Shiva himself. He does it for love or to uplift the world. Knowledge is one of the best gifts one can give to another. If it is self-knowledge, it is the best of all gifts. Initiating a seeker into the path of liberation and giving him the right knowledge to achieve is the best gift a guru can give to his students. It is also the highest penance for a righteous cause in deference to the Shiva-tattva (pure consciousness), which is now the essential nature of the enlightened teacher (Jangama). United with Shiva as the source of all, he becomes the giver of self-knowledge to qualified people who abide in him, worship him, and prove their resolve to be absorbed in him without duality. Those who attain self-knowledge through union with him are also qualified to pass it on to others according to their discretion. A self-realized Shiva yogi is the best guru one can have. Knowledge naturally flows from him, just as light radiates from the sun or fragrance from a flower. Since the power and consciousness of Shiva illuminate him, his words and speech have a purifying effect on those who follow him and absorb his teachings without doubt and criticism. With his knowledge and potencies, he can grant them the knowledge of liberation, protect them from evil, and remove from them the ill effects of their karma arising from the darkness of their delusion, egoism and attachments, attraction and aversion, duality and divisions, etc. Self-knowledge is the supreme gift a yogi can give to others in the mortal world. Only a self-realized Shiva yogi is perfectly qualified to do it.

3-29 yo'vipastho jñāhetuśca

He who is established in the Avipa Shaktis is the cause of knowledge.

Avi means sheep or ignorant beings who are enveloped by impurities and exist in their animal (pasu) state. Avipa refers to the array of goddesses (Shakti chakra), such as Maheswari, who control the avis by keeping them in their impure state of egoism, attachments, and delusion. The avipas are of four types: the khechari goddesses of the "kha" group who control the mind, the gochari goddesses who preside over the internal organs and control them, the dikchari goddesses who preside over the sense organs and organs of action and control them, and the bhuchari goddesses who control the elements in the body. The yogi who brings them under his control and becomes established in them as their Lord (pati) in union with the Self or Shiva is known as avipastha. Since he is established in pure consciousness, knowledge is inherent to him and naturally flows from him. Hence, he is the most reliable source of teaching and illumination to those who approach him for self-knowledge and liberation. He is the right one to impart to them the gift of knowledge and lift them from the darkness of their minds and bodies by introducing to them the secrets of pure consciousness and how to attain it. As the Lord of the Shaktis in his body and their bodies, with the power to remove their darkness and ignorance, he lights the lamp of knowledge and illumination in them and becomes the cause of their pure knowledge (jnana hetu).

3-30 *svaśakti pracayo'sya viśvam*

The universe is the outflow or expansion of his own Shaktis.

The universe is an outflow or outward expansion of Shiva's Shaktis, who participate in creation as the reigning goddesses of the deluded world of ignorant beings. It arises from his will and force and is filled with his essence. The avipastha who has attained oneness with Shiva and gained the lordship of his Avipa Shaktis sees the world in the same manner as filled with his own illumination and power. He not only cognizes the world in the unified state as a play of his own making but also possesses the power, just as Shiva, to create new worlds in the subtle planes and breathe life into them according to his will. The world is the eye of Shiva. It is filled with knowledge, consciousness, and illumination, which continuously flow from him, and it exists as long as his gaze is fixed upon it. What he sees or cognizes in his universal and acentric vision is what happens or manifests because there is no duality between his will and his manifestation or between the seer (Shiva) and the seen (the objective reality). It is the same Parashakti who rules over the universe as his inseparable companion and executes his will for his enjoyment. As this sutra alludes, one can say the same about the avipastha who has conquered his limited beingness and merged in Shiva. He may not have the same scale of power and reach as Shiva, the Supreme Lord, since he is bound to his body, but he possesses those powers as seeds in his consciousness.

3-31 stithilayau

Preservation and destruction also.

Just as the enlightened yogi who attained the pure consciousness and aloneness of Shiva possesses the power to create, he possesses the power to preserve and destroy. The whole creation is filled with Shiva's energies (Shaktis). They are responsible for all actions and movements as a part of his Play, including creation, preservation, concealment, revelation, and destruction. All the worlds arise from his seeing, continue as long as he fixes his gaze upon them, and cease to exist as soon as he withdraws his attention and goes into himself. All things that manifest in creation arise and subside in him only since they are filled with his illumination and moved by his Shaktis. Therefore, they exist as long as he illuminates them, witnessing the Shaktis playing hide and seek among themselves, and disappear as soon as he withdraws them and the Shaktis into himself and becomes absorbed in himself. These powers are limited in ordinary people since the

Shaktis in them are veiled and limited by Maya. Hence, they have to struggle to manifest their thoughts or fulfill their desires, in which they do not always succeed or stay in control. It is not the same with self-realized yogis, who are firmly established in the supreme consciousness of Shiva. They possess the same potencies as Shiva, although on a limited scale and not absolutely, which they can unleash at will. However, yogis, even with those limited powers, rarely exist on earth since complete and absolute union or oneness with Shiva in a mortal body is almost impossible to achieve. Still, with whatever perfection and potencies they have, the Siddhas, or adept yogis, can do the world a lot of good through their thoughts and actions.

3-32 tat pravrttāvapyanirāsah samvettrbhāvāt

Even during such outward prvrittis, the state of the pure knower is unbroken.

A Siddha's one-pointed attention and continuous awareness do not waver even when he is engaged in actions or when his mind is in its outward mode (prvritti). He remains firmly established in the pure consciousness of Shiva as the knower, witnessing all the drama that unfolds before him enacted by his own Shaktis. That which is indestructible is never lost. The same holds for the consciousness of the yogi who has attained Shiva. It is never lost for him, nor can it be disturbed or broken by any power. Shiva tattva becomes his very nature. Even when he engages in outward activities such as creation and destruction, his internal state of blissful turya, oneness with Shiva, and illuminated consciousness remains the same. He is unaffected by what he does or does not do. His equanimity as the knower (samvettrah bhava) prevails in all conditions and circumstances because it neither depends nor arises from external conditions but from his inseparable unity with Shiva's pure consciousness. His ego arising from his mind-body awareness does not participate in it or contribute to it, nor can it in any way connect to him or distract him when he is absorbed in the uninterrupted flow of turya. In the presence of the Self, his tattvas remain subdued and silent. The pure consciousness that illuminates his knowledge and awareness is self-knowing, independent, permanent, indestructible, undisturbed, and immutable. The Shaktis who reside in him also radiate his purity and intelligence. Therefore, the weak condition (avara prasara), which arises in many yogis and disturbs them in the middle of turya, does not arise in him. Illuminated by his pure Self and united with his radiant energies, he remains detached and equal, unaffected by external or internal causes and conditions. The world and his body cease to exert any influence upon him. Therefore, when he engages in actions, he remains equal to all the pairs of opposites. He may project and withdraw things with his consciousness, but those outward and inward actions (prvritti and nivrttti) by which he makes things and appear and disappear do not disturb the continuity or stability of his transcendental turya or his absorption in it.

3-33 sukha duhkhayorbahirmananam
Thinks that pain and pleasure are external.

There are two types of consciousness in each of us: pure consciousness and consciousness arising from the body. When the two are mixed up, one experiences egoism, desires, and the delusion that the mind and body constitute the Self. A yogi overcomes this problem by separating himself from his body and abiding in his pure consciousness, which has no traces of body awareness or body-related desires and attachments. He lives in the body without being connected to it and becomes free from it to qualify as jivanmukta and an embodiment of pure consciousness. In that state, he is not disturbed by pain and pleasure since he views them as external to him or internal to his body, from which he has already disconnected himself and does not feel any attachment to it. People experience dualities such as pain and pleasure or heat and cold, and all bodily sensations and experiences as if they are happening to them and in them because of their association and attachment with their bodies. For them, such experiences are real and internal since they lack discernment and clarity and identify themselves with their minds and bodies. Thus deluded, they internalize their perceptions and experiences and feel disturbed by them. Due to their attachments and identification, sometimes, they feel disturbed by others' suffering also, even if they have no physical connection with it. It is not the case with the yogis who overcome their delusion, renounce their attachment and identification with their minds and bodies, and abide in the pure consciousness or the auspicious state of Shiva that is completely free from the consciousness and modifications arising from perceptions, sensations, feelings, etc. Since they dissolve their egos and all other bodily impurities and attain pure consciousness over which the Shaktis of the body have no control, they do not feel disturbed by what happens in the world or their minds and bodies. For them, all that arises from and is related to the body constitutes the not-self or the objective reality. Therefore, they remain stable even when they are actively engaged with the outside world. Just as the Self is not connected to the mind and body in which it exists, the yogis are disconnected from their bodies and the world. It is not that pain and pleasure do not arise in them. They do not react as they detach themselves from all the Prakriti tattvas, cultivate indifference and endurance, and maintain uninterrupted and continuous focus upon their Shiva tattva or pure consciousness. When suffering or disturbances arise in their bodies (the Field), they see them as vrittis that arise in them due to their inherent nature or the play of Maya. Without reacting to them or making any effort to control them or mitigate them, they remain unmoved and absorbed.

3-34 tadvimuktaslu kevalī

Becoming free, he remains alone.

Kevali is the one who has attained kaivalya, the state of aloneness. His aloneness is not the depressing kind of loneliness, but the state of final liberation, which is filled with the bliss and illumination of supreme consciousness in which there is no place or scope for suffering, duality or delusion. It arises from the state of nonduality, when a yogi perceives only one, indivisible reality everywhere and in everything as himself or his essential state. Free from all attachments, associations, dependence, conditions and dualities, he becomes self-existent, self-luminous, independent and self-knowing. In him the idea of renunciation reaches its culmination, whereby he becomes disentangled not only from the world, his mind and body, thoughts, feelings and emotions but also from his past lives, latent impressions, memories and knowledge of wakeful and dream states. By remaining fully absorbed in pure consciousness and acknowledging it as his sole reality and true self, he becomes equal to the world around him. With the destruction of causes, when the ever changing, objective reality (this, idam) ceases to create ripples in his consciousness, his independent and transcendental self (That, tat) remains as one (kevala).

3-35 mohapratisamhatastu karmātmā

The deluded one is verily karmatma.

Deluded beings identify themselves with their names and forms and live in the world accordingly, performing desire-ridden actions and accumulating karma, which produces pain and suffering, and bonds (pasas) that are difficult to overcome. Their lives and destinies, and their minds and bodies arise from karma and are made up of karma only. Thus, they are children of karma and truly qualify as karmatmas or beings of karma. Theirs is the state of not knowing who they are or their true nature as beings of pure consciousness due to egoism, desires, and delusion. In that state, beings remain in their outward mode, deluded by māya, as they extend their minds and senses into the world and perform actions to satisfy their needs and desires and accumulate material things. Because of that, they remain bound to samsara, oblivious of their essential nature which is pure consciousness. In contrast, enlightened yogis are untouched by karma. They abide in pure consciousness, detached from their physical nature or their minds and bodies and all the impurities associated with them. Their consciousness shines with purity, perfection, and sameness in oneness with Shiva or the Self. Being pure (suddha atma) and firmly established in unified consciousness, which is kept illuminated and stabilized by their continuous contemplation and adoration of Shiva, untainted and untouched by desires, the gunas, and karma, they remain free from the hold of Maya and all the Shaktis that work for her. As the lords of their minds and bodies and firmly established in oneness and sameness, they remain pure whether they perform actions or not or live amidst impurities. Thus, an adept yogi (siddha) is verily a Shivatma who has installed

Shiva in the temple of his body as his very consciousness and his true embodiment.

3-36 bheda tiraskāre sargāntara karmatvam

Upon discarding the duality, the power to manifest another creation.

Duality exists at various levels. The most important duality is the duality between the body and pure consciousness, which has no traces of the body or Prakriti and the consciousness associated with it. For success on this path, a yogi has to renounce his body, acknowledge his pure consciousness as his essential nature, and, through that, establish a direct and lasting connection with the absolute state of Shiva. The beingness, which arises from karma and envelops the Self (pure consciousness) as a mass of impurity, is a degraded condition because it veils the power and potencies of the pure Self and keeps the jiva deluded, divided, and distracted. The being who is made up of karma (karmatma), created and continued by karma, and is bound to it through prarabdha is limited by his impurities, which veil his powers to create, preserve, and destroy or ability to control time, order, place, circumstances, etc. Due to the influence of māya and the karma of his past, he does not have much freedom or independence to exercise his will or create anything other than what they permit. Therefore, as a prisoner of his fate and circumstances, he can only create what has already been destined for him. It is not the case with a yogi who has transcended duality and division and is absorbed in the undifferentiated pure consciousness. He can manifest any reality according to his free will, which is independent and unbound. Invoking his unlimited powers, he can change the course of things or the world itself. With his spontaneous knowledge of mantras, spells, and Mantra Shaktis, he can change people's lives too. As the lord of all and Shiva himself, in the state of non-duality, he can even grant freedom and powers to others to manifest their wish and will or fulfill their wishes. When a yogi attains Shivatvam, Shakti follows him dutifully and settles in his consciousness. When you become one with Shiva, without duality or distinction, everything becomes possible as you become the lord of all the Shaktis in the universe.

3-37 karanaśaktih svato'nubhavāt

Karana-Shakti through self-experience.

Karana Shakti is the ability to cause or manifest desired outcomes. It may mean creative, causative, or instrumental power or the power that is inherent to the organs in the body. In ignorant people, it remains limited. In the deluded state, karana Shakti is bound to karma and natural limitations. It arises from karma and leads to karma and bondage. Thus, the deluded ones remain bound to the chain of karma, with little or no power to change it unless they fundamentally change their ways to become united with their pure nature, which is hidden in them behind a veil of Maya. The Self or pure consciousness is always the cause. It is never an effect or product, unlike the mind and body, which are productions or produced by one's actions, chance, or fate. The Self is endowed with unlimited power to cause or create (Karana-Shakti) desired outcomes without any external help or support. Those who become absorbed in it due to an uninterrupted connection with Shiva develop a similar power. By the grace of Shiva, they become endowed with unlimited power to cause or create, with which they can manifest reality by thought or intention without physical means or dependence upon their bodies. The creative or causative power (Karana Shakti) in adept yogis arises from their inseparable and continuous connection with Shiva, with whom they are united without duality at the level of consciousness while remaining detached from their bodies. In them, the triple Shaktis (Iccha, Jnana, and Kriya) remain under their control and follow their will since their consciousness is illuminated by Shiva's pure consciousness without duality. Once they establish the unending flow of the transcendental turya into them through that connection, that power is never lost. This is not the case with the ignorant beings. Their causative power is controlled by Maya-Shaktis and their essential nature, as determined by their gunas. Therefore, although they may appear to have the freedom to engage in actions and exercise their free will, in truth, they play out what has already been destined for them by their karma, fate, and chance. They cannot change their lives or their destinies without Shiva's grace or without attaining liberation.

3-38 tripadādyanuprānanam

The three states are energized with prana by the first.

This sutra suggests how a yogi can generate happiness from within without seeking pleasure or happiness from the outside world. He can do so by drawing the bliss of turya from his pure Self, the first (adibhuta), into the three states of consciousness, namely the wakeful, dream, and deep sleep states, or into his mind, body, and mind-body consciousness. He can also extend it into the beginning, middle and end of any activity which he performs by pouring in the bliss of pure consciousness. A Shiva yogi who has attained oneness with Shiva can do it in any condition and at any time, both externally and internally, in wakeful and meditative states, since he can sustain the blissful state (turya) of pure consciousness by maintaining a continuous connection with Shiva, envisioning him within himself and everywhere with uninterrupted oneness. He does not have to recall or remember it since it remains with him in all the four states. However, a yogi who has not attained liberation can only do it intermittently in deep meditative states, remembering and strengthening moments of happiness or pleasure he experienced from mundane actions, such as eating, sleeping, sexual union, etc. The happiness or the pleasure that arises in the beginning, middle, and end phases of such mundane experiences is but turya only, although its purity and intensity are lost, diluted, or even polluted by Maya and the grossness of the body. Knowing this, the yogi uses them to sustain turya-like states in normal circumstances and keeps himself filled with positive and radiant energies. He keeps energizing himself with memories of pleasant experiences and blissful moments. From this sutra, we learn that spiritual practice does not have to be depressing. One can generate happiness and bliss internally without depending upon external objects and circumstances. The next sutra suggests that this practice should not be confined to meditative inquiry only.

3-39 cittasthitivat śarīra karana bāhyesu

As in the mind, so in the body, senses, and external objects.

Just as the bliss of turya is brought into the three states of consciousness, a yogi can do the same in the wakeful state when his mind is actively engaged with the objective world. He can do it by withdrawing his mind and senses and contemplating upon the nature of turya. With his mind fixed upon the bliss of that transcendental state or pure consciousness, he can gradually soak his consciousness (chitta) with it - while remaining detached from his mind and body and keeping his desires and gunas subdued - and drive away all traces of darkness. Whether he is awake or at rest, he can extend it and experience it in his gross and subtle bodies, organs, tattvas, thoughts, and memories. He can also extend it to the whole perceptual world and see it filling and illuminating everything in him and around him. With its continued and perseverant practice, he can fill his gross and subtle bodies with the power and consciousness (chaitanya Shakti) of Shiva, which is natural (sahaja) to the transcendental state of turya. Skillful yogis who practice it develop the ability to rekindle the bliss of turya at will in whatever form or object they wish to experience in a state of nonduality. From this and the previous sutra, we can infer that adept yogis can transform mundane states into blissful experiences by pouring into them the delightful states of transcendence. In doing so, they do not lose their energies due to exhaustion, overuse, or enervation, which is the case with ordinary people, but hold them steady and keep replenishing them from within.

3-40 abhilāsādbahirgatih samvāhyasya (sambahyasya)

Due to desires the samvāhya is outbound.

Samvahya means an ignorant and deluded being (pasu or avi) who is bound to the cycle of births and deaths and keeps wandering in the mortal world from one birth to another. Under the influence of māya and in a state of delusion and ignorance, he is increasingly drawn to worldly life and to the enjoyment of worldly pleasures. Hence, he remains outbound, oblivious of his true nature, with his mind and senses constantly dwelling upon sense objects. As he engages in desire-ridden actions due to attraction and aversion, his impure nature grows in strength and grossness, which leads to suffering and repeated births in bodies that are impure and filled with the causes of bondage. His suffering arises mainly because of his preoccupation with the objective realm. A yogi learns this at an early stage in his practice and develops a distaste for the world, knowing that it is the cause of delusion and suffering. He cultivates discernment and withdraws his attention from it to remain detached, indifferent, and absorbed in the contemplation of Shiva. As he overcomes duality and achieves oneness (kaivalyam) with him, he discovers the fountain of bliss within himself and loses all interest in the pleasures and attractions of the external world. When he turns his attention upon the world, it is for a higher cause, but not to fulfill any desires or gain anything. The abhilasha (intention) of a deluded being is driven by desires, whereas in a self-realized yogi, it is pure and arises from his independent, free will. Some versions contain the word sambahyasya instead of samvahyasya. It means that the outbound intention and attention of a yogi is always equal or the same, due to nonduality.

3-41
tadārūdhapramitestatkṣayājjīvasaṃkṣayah

Fixing the consciousness in it and removing desires, the jiva is dissolved.

By destroying desires and firmly fixing the blissful turya in the consciousness and the body through the practices which are described in the previous sutras, the adept yogi renders the jiva in him ineffective and inconsequential. His limited beingness (anava) and consciousness cease to exert any influence upon him. When we say that the jiva is dissolved, it does not mean that the body of the jiva disappears or is destroyed. It means that when the body of a yogi becomes pure and self-illumined, it carries no importance to him as it ceases to disturb or distract him. As he becomes detached from it and establishes his attention on Shiva tattva, he loses awareness of it and lives as if he has no physical body. Once he is firmly established in the natural state of the Self, his dependence upon his mind and body also comes to an end. The body is a formation around the Self, which is both gross and subtle. In the embodied state, one is never free from it. Even upon death, a part of it accompanies the Self to the next birth, carrying a print of the predominant impressions and desires of past lives. The vishaya vasanas (attachments to worldly objects) survive death. It is why self-purification is an important first step in liberation. After purifying his mind and body and removing cravings and attachments, when a yogi enters turya and soaks his whole being with pure consciousness, his limited beingness (jivabhav) and ego (anava) are suppressed, and the mental formations in his mind disappear. With his ego crushed under the feet of Shiva, as symbolized in the images of Nataraja, he attains the nature of Shiva (shivabhāv) and becomes a free soul in the body (jivanmukta) with unlimited knowledge, awareness, and potencies. Since he is free from desires, his actions do not bind him, whether he performs them with or without any desire or intention.

3-42 bhūtakañcukī tadā vimukto bhūyah patisamah parah

Then, freed from the gross and subtle, he becomes equal to the Supreme lord.

When a yogi is fully established in the natural state (sahaja vidya) of the supreme consciousness and ceases to be body-centric, he becomes equal to Shiva in a living body. Bhuta kanchuki refers to the gross and subtle bodies, which are made up of 36 tattvas and envelop the Self in three consecutive layers, namely kanchuki (super subtle), puryastaka (subtle), and sthula (gross). The body is the main obstacle. Filled with māya and other impurities, it veils the illumination of the Self, which is known as Shiva tattva or pure (suddha) tattva. Its essential nature is eternal and indestructible, pure consciousness filled with blissful turya. In ordinary beings, the impurities of the mind and body suppress Shivabhav (divinity) and fill them with jivabhav (beingness). When a yogi enters turya and merges into pure consciousness, the opposite happens. His divinity outshines his beingness. His body, freed from impurities and subdued, becomes a temple for Shiva, the Supreme Lord, who dwells in it as its sole support and presiding deity, untouched by its vrittis and prvrittis. Although he is still embodied in it, he does not feel any attachment to it. With blissful, pure consciousness as his natural state, firmly established in the absolute supreme reality (parama tattva) of oneness, and unbound to his physical nature, he lives in the world as Shiva, performing his bodily functions (sharira vrittis) as a penance (vratam).

3-43 naisargikah prānasambandhah

The connection with prana is innate or natural.

When a yogi becomes free from the influence of his body and lives as if it does not exist, does it mean that he does not have to breathe or eat food to keep his body alive? Does his body require any maintenance or support? Clearly, the answer is no. Liberation is for the soul, not for the body. The Self is independent and self-existent, but the body is dependent and destructible. It needs nourishment, care, and protection as long as the Self exists in it. Just as Shiva takes care of his ignorant devotees, a jivanmukta has to take care of his body with the same care and compassion. Therefore, even after a yogi casts off his attachments and desires and severs his connection with his subtle and gross bodies, he still has to maintain a connection with his physical self as a part of his prarabdha karma and keep nourishing it with food, water, prana, etc. Although he is free from his body and the impurities arising in it, the tattvas in his body still require nourishment to perform their natural functions. Hence, as stated in a previous sutra, a yogi has to engage in body-related karma as penance in deference to the tattvas and the

Shaktis who reside in him and serve him with devotion. However, his connection with prana becomes innate, which means it flows within him continuously, even if he does not draw it from the outside. In other words, he can control, suspend, or hold the prana within himself indefinitely and remain alive without breathing. Since he purifies his body and clears the blockages in his nadis to facilitate the free flow of prana through them, he can sustain himself even with a limited supply of prana. He can also do it by controlling the flow of prana in them. This has been demonstrated by many yogis in the past and even scientifically.

3-44 nāsikāntarmadhya samyamāt kimatra savyāpasavya sausumnesu

After controlling the breath in the middle of the nostrils, in the left, right, and middle nadis, what else is to be done?

According to this sutra, the height of self-control and the culmination of Anavopaya is complete freedom and independence from the body and its organs and functions. One of the visible signs of this is the ability to suspend or hold breath in his nostrils (nasikantara madhya) and in the three main nadis: Ida, Pingala, and Sushumna. This is a sign that the yogi has succeeded in attaining blissful turya (pure consciousness) as his natural condition in wakeful, dream, and deep sleep states and reached the highest goal of oneness with Shiva. For him, no further spiritual practice is required since he has attained Shiva consciousness as his essential nature and reached the end of his journey. The nadis exist in the body like an intricate web of energy channels. They carry prana. Since they are subtle and invisible, they cannot physically be located. They are perceptible through the inner eye only when one develops subtle vision. They carry prana (a subtle form of energy drawn from outside through breath) to various organs, nerve centers, and chakras in the body and provide them with the much-needed vital energy that is necessary to keep the body in balance. All the nadis in the body, whose number is in thousands, coalesce into three principal nadis, namely the Ida on the left, the Pingala on the right, and the Sushumna in the middle. Ida and Pingala are known as Savya and Apasavya. Sushumna is the middle one, Madhya. They are located in the back of the body along the spine. Each of them plays an important role in the vital functions of the body, in the distribution of energy, and in the spiritual transformation of the initiate. The prana that flows in them is illuminated by the twin presence of Shiva and Shakti, known as Samvit and Vimarsh. Samvit is pure consciousness, and vimarsh is pure energy. Together, they illuminate prana and facilitate its forward and onward flow. By focusing upon it and dissolving in it, a yogi enters the supreme state of self-absorption known as nirvyutthana (freedom from neural excitement). When he attains that exalted state through samyama (control), there is nothing else that needs to be done.

3-45 bhūyah syāt pratimīlanam

There will be a reversal to the original state again.

At the end of the great journey of self-purification and transformation, the Self (consciousness of the jiva) returns to its original and pristine state of undivided and indestructible pure consciousness of Supreme Shiva. Creation is a projection of the Self, the original cause. Someday, it will revert or dissolve into its cause. So is the beingness of a jiva. It is a temporary formation of Shaktis around the Self, which results in its bondage and suffering in the mortal world. When it is liberated, it returns to its original or natural state of pure knowing (sahaja vidya) endowed with the triple energies, namely Iccha, Jnana, and Kriya Shaktis. The Self is never tainted by the impurities that prevail around it as its body and objective consciousness that is formed by the activity of the internal organ (antahkarana). There is no loss or change for the Self when it is trapped in the tattvas and no gain when it is liberated from them. Liberation is similar to waking up from a long sleep or a long dream. When a yogi wakes up in a true sense from it, he remembers who he is and returns to his absolute state of pure consciousness. This sutra contains the implied assurance that however fallen and impure beings may be, they can hope for liberation and return to their pure state either by their effort or by the grace of Shiva and Shakti. The jivatmas are never separate from them. Even in their ignorant state, although they are clouded by impurities, they all are still emanations of Shiva deep within their clouded consciousness. Their connection with him is never lost. Therefore, they can always return to their original state by mere remembrance or awakening, which may happen through divine intervention, the intervention of Shaktis, or personal effort. In that journey, the yogi gains nothing because, as the pure Self, he is complete and has nothing to gain. All that he has to do is to remove the veil of impurities and obstructions that keep him from knowing his oneness with Shiva and Shakti (shivatvam) and regain his original knowledge or awareness. When he returns to that supreme state, he will never again relapse into the impure and deluded state of a jiva.

Aum Tat Sat

Shiva Sutras – Free Translation

Part 1 - Śāmbhavopāya

1-1 caitanyamātmā: Chaitanyam is the Self.

The self is the essence of all. It is pure consciousness, knowledge, intelligence, awareness, vitality, and sensation which pervades the whole existence.

1-2 jñānam bandhah: Knowledge is bondage.

Worldly knowledge, which arises from the activities of the mind and senses and is infused with Maya, is the source of bondage.

1-3 yonivarga kalāśarīram: The body is (an assembly of) womb class tattvas such as kala.

The body is made up of womb-born tattvas such as Kala, Niyati, ego, mind, intelligence, senses, etc.

1-4 jñānādhisthāna mātrikā: Mātrika is the support of knowledge.

The letters, letter-forms, and sounds in the Sanskrit alphabet are filled with the knowledge and power of Shakti.

1-5 udyamo bhairavah: The uprising of Bhairavah.

The illumination of Bhairava (Brahman or Shiva) manifests in the silence between two thoughts or two consecutive movements of the mind during contemplation.

1-6 śakticakrasandhāne viśvasamhārah: *The destroyer of the world, wielding Shakti chakra.*

Wielding the power hidden in the Shakti chakras, one should look upon the objective world as nonexistent or immaterial.

1-7 jāgrat-svapna-susupta-bhede turyābhogasambhavah: *Turya enjoyment can arise in between jagrat, svapna, and susupta.*

Turya enjoyment is possible in the transitional period between jagrat, svapna, and susupta, just as you are falling asleep or entering a dream or waking up from deep sleep.

1-8 jñānam jagrat: The wakeful state is knowledge.

The knowledge which arises from the wakeful consciousness is jagrat knowledge. It is essentially perceptual knowledge, subject to duality, delusion, egoism, division, separation, and ignorance.

1-9 svapno vikalpāh: The dream state is vikalpa.

The knowledge which arises from dream (svapna) consciousness is vikalpa, imaginary or fantasy knowledge arising in duality. It is also subject to the influence of Maya and delusion.

1-10 aviveko māyāsausuptam: Susupta is indistinct and deluded.

The knowledge which arises in deep sleep (susupta) is indistinct and bereft of knowledge and intelligence. It is completely filled with Maya. Hence, nothing can be known about it.

1-11 tritayabhoktā vīreśah: The enjoyer of the three is the heroic lord, Shiva.

As the lord of the mind and senses, Shiva is the enjoyer of all three states, the one who remains awake, dreams, and falls asleep in the body in the embodied state as a part of his play, remaining untouched by any of them.

1-12 vismayo yogabhūmikāh: Wondrous, the states of yoga.

Wondrous and blissful is the state of turya, the transcendental state that intermittently arises during the practice of yoga, filling one with amazing feelings.

1-13 icchā śaktirumā kumārī: Uma Kumari is Iccha Shakti (the power of desire).

Uma Kumari is your willpower. She is a virgin goddess who should not be used for selfish enjoyment or to fulfil your desires. If you do, you will be subject to her anger and incur karma and sin.

1-14 dṛśyam śarīram: The visible, the body is.

The body is the visible self. It houses the true self, which is invisible. You should not consider your body to be the Self just because you perceive it and become attached to it. Know that it is just an outer covering.

1-15 hrdaye cittasamghaṭṭād dṛśyasvāpnadarśanam: When the chitta is gathered in the heart, the seeing of the visible and the dream (worlds).

When you purify your consciousness, which flows through the nadis, the heart, and the chakras, you will discern the truth about the wakeful and dream worlds and see them as they are without being deluded by them.

1-16 śuddhatattvasandhānād vā apaśuśaktih: By meditating on the pure tattva, the absence of animal nature.

By meditating upon the pure Self, you can cleanse your mind and body, suppress the Maya Shaktis, and overcome your animal nature, which is the cause of delusion, egoism, ignorance, and bondage.

1-17 vitarka ātmajñānam: By contemplation, knowledge of the Self.

Through contemplative, meditative, and systematic inquiry into the nature of the Self with discernment, separating what the Self is and what the Self is not, you will gain the knowledge of the Self

1-18 lokānandah samādhisukham: The bliss of the world and the bliss of samadhi.:

The bliss of the world and the bliss of samadhi are the same for an awakened and self-realized yogi. Even when he is enjoying the pleasures of the world, he remains established in the bliss of self-absorption.

1-19 śaktisandhāne śarīrotpattih

With meditation upon Shakti, one attains the power to create a new being with a body, transform an existing body, or appear in different bodies at the same.

1-20 bhūtasandhāna bhūtaprthaktva viśvasamghattāh: The power to unite or separate elements assembles the world.

Through practice, a yogi develops the power to unite or separate elements and bring together various things to create a world out of them.

1-21 śuddhavidyodayāccakreśatva siddhih: With the onset of shuddha vidya, the lordship of chakras is accomplished.

With the onset of seeing the pure Self in all, which is known as Shuddha Vidya, one attains the siddhi, or power of lordship, over the energy centers called Chakras in the body.

1-22 mahāhradānusandhānānmantravīryānubhavah: By reaching the great lake, the experience of mantra virya.

By reaching the great lake of pure consciousness wherein resides the great Parashakti called the Maha Hrda, one experiences the awakening of Shaktis who are hidden in the sacred letters and sounds.

Part 2 – Śāktopāya

2-1 cittah mantrah: The mind is the mantra.

The consciousness (chitta) of a self-realized yogi is as effective and capable as a mantra, with the power to invoke and manifest the Shaktis who reside in it just as mantras can manifest the Shaktis who are hidden in them.

2-2 prayatnah sādhakah: Willful effort for success.

Through willful and pointed effort, a yogi succeeds in invoking and becoming the Lord of the Shaktis who are hidden in his consciousness and in the mantras upon which he meditates with one-pointedness.

2-3 vidyāśarīrasattā mantrarahasyam: The power of vidya sariram, the secret of the mantra.

The secret of the mantra is its body, which has knowledge as its moving force. A yogi who illuminates his chitta and mental body with pure knowledge develops a similar power and gains lordship over the Mantra Shaktis.

2-4 garbhe cittavikāso'viśista vidyāsvapnah: From the flowering of chitta in the womb of māya arises dreamlike indistinct knowledge.

From the flowering of the chitta in an impure body that is filled with Maya, there arises dreamlike indistinct knowledge with limited powers.

2-5 vidyāsamutthāne svābhāvike khecarī śivāvasthā: With the natural advent of vidya, khechari and Shiva state.

With the natural advent of vidya, there is illumination of the consciousness with khechari and the attainment of Shiva state and pure knowledge.

2-6 gururupāyah: The guru is the means.

The guru is the means to overcome the impurities of the mind and body, awaken the Mantra Shaktis who reside in the matrkas and attain the pure consciousness of the Self.

2-7 mātrkācakrasambodhah: Matrka chakra is known.

With the help of an adept guru, a yogi gains the knowledge of matrka chakra and how to harness the Mantra Shaktis that are hidden in the sound forms of speech for self-purification and self-realization.

2-8 śarīram havih: The body is a sacrificial offering.

The body is the oblation in the sacrifice of self-purification in which the impurities of the mind and body are poured into the fire of knowledge as an offering to the Shaktis who participate in it.

2-9 jñānam annam: Knowledge is food.

In the sacrifice of self-purification, impure knowledge, which arises from the activities of the mind and senses in the wakeful, dream, and deep sleep states and which causes ignorance, delusion, and bondage is the food for the ego. It should be offered to the Self in the sacrifice of self-purification

2-10 vidyāsamhāre taduttha svapna darsanam: When knowledge is destroyed, the seeing of the dream.

When the knowledge is thus destroyed in the sacrifice of self-purification, the yogi experiences the world as a dream of Shiva and his body as a formation. He realizes their illusory nature and becomes established in pure knowledge.

Part 3- Anavopāya

3-1 ātmā cittam: Atma is chitta.

By nature, the embodied Self is also consciousness only. However, it is limited and impure due to its association with the tattvas in the body and the actions of Maya, who veils its illumination and purity.

3-2 jñānam bandhah: Knowledge (arising from the impure chitta) is binding.

The knowledge that arises from the internal-organ (the mind, the senses, intelligence and ego) is binding because it causes duality, delusion, egoism, attachments and bondage to samsara.

3-3 kalādīnām tattvānām aviveko māyā: Ignorance of tattvas, such as kala, etc., is māya.

The ignorance of various tattvas, such as kala, etc., make up the body. They are responsible for suffering and bondage, and for the jivas mistaking them as the real Self; this is the delusion.

3-4 śarīre samhārah kalānām : In the body, destroying kala, etc.

One should engage in the purification of the body by destroying the impurities of the tattvas, such as Kala.

3-5 nādī samhāra bhūtajaya bhūtakaivalya bhūtaprithaktvāni: By stopping the nadis, conquest of elements, dissolution of elements and separation of elements.

By dissolving the impurities in the nadis and removing their blockages, one gains the power to control, dissolve, and separate the elements in oneself and in creation.

3-6 mohāvaranāt siddhih: Siddhi, while still being veiled by moha.

One may gain supernatural powers through nadi samhara, bhuta jaya, etc., while still being veiled by delusion, but not the knowledge of the pure tattva or self-realization.

3-7 mohajayād anantābhogāt sahajavidyājayah: With the unquestionable conquest of māya, the triumph of sahajavidya.

With unquestionable conquest of māya, one enters the supreme state of Shiva and gains true knowledge (sahajavidya), which is natural to the Self.

3-8 jāgrad dvitīyakarah: Jagrat becomes secondary.

When a yogi is firmly established in the pure knowledge of the Self, the wakeful world becomes secondary to him, like a ray or an extension or projection within himself.

3-9 nartaka ātmā: The Self is the Dance Master.

He sees himself as the dance master or actor on a stage set by himself, playing different roles in different forms for his own enjoyment.

3-10 rango'ntarātmā: The stage is the inner Self.

The inner Self is the stage where he enacts the dance drama.

3-11 prekśakānīndriyāni: The sense organs are the spectators.

The sense organs are the spectators in that dance drama.

3-12 dhīvaśāt sattvasiddhih: By controlling dhi, purity is attained.

By controlling intelligence (dhi) and with discernment, using the right means with right knowledge, purity is attained.

3-13 siddhah svatantrabhāvah: The state of freedom is attained.

By merging with Shiva, the yogi attains the freedom to exercise his free will, know and act independently.

3-14.1 yathā tatra tathānyatra: As there, so elsewhere.

As in the body, so elsewhere, a yogi enjoys unobstructed, unrestrained freedom.

3-14.2 visargasvābhāvyād abahih sthitestatsthitih: What has spread out is not external but internally located.

For a self-realized yogi what has spread out or exists outside as his body or the world is not external, but internal only as an aspect of himself and his pure consciousness.

3-15 bījāvadhānam: Concentration on the seed.

With his mind firmly fixed upon Shiva, a yogi should practice concentration on the seed or the cause to cultivate purity.

3-16 āsanasthah sukham hrade nimajjati: Abiding in asana, effortlessly sinks into the lake.

Abiding in concentration, with his mind firmly fixed upon the Self by the power of Shakti, he should effortlessly sink into the lake of pure consciousness.

3-17 svamātrā nirmānam āpādayati: With his Shakti, he manifests creation.

With Parashakti who is now an inseparable part of him, the self-realized yogi manifests creation.

3-18 vidyā avināśe janma vināśah: With the indestructible knowledge, the end of birth.

With the dawn of indestructible knowledge, there is the destruction of the causes of bondage to the cycle of births and deaths.

3-19 kavargādisu māheśvaryādyāh paśumātarah: Mahesvari and others of the "ka" group of Shaktis are mothers of pashus.

Mahesvari and others of the "ka" group of Shaktis become mothers of pashus or beings who are born with animal nature, veiled by Maya.

3-20 trisu caturtham tailavadāsecyam: Into the three should be dropped the fourth like oil.

In the three states of wakeful, dream, and deep sleep states, the bliss of the fourth state of turya should be dropped like oil.

3-21 magnah svacittena praviśet: Becoming absorbed, let him enter through his own consciousness.

Through mental absorption (chitta magna) by abiding in the steady state of contemplation (asana), one should reach the Self through one's own consciousness (svachitta).

3-22 prāna samācāre samadarśanam: With the slow movement of prana arises the seeing of sameness.

With the slow movement of prana in the body, there arises the seeing of sameness or the same Self in everyone.

3-23 madhye'vara prasarah: In the middle, avara prasarah.

A disconnected state of enjoyment and duality arises in the middle of turya when attention or control is lost or weakened.

3-24 mātrāsu svapratyaya sandhāne nastasya punarutthānam: By uniting the Self with the objects and the like, the loss is regained.

By reconnection oneself to the objects and the like and finding oneself in them in the state of nonduality, the loss is regained.

3-25 śivatulyo jāyate: He becomes Shiva-like.

In the unified state of illuminated consciousness, the yogi becomes pure and resplendent, just like Shiva.

3-26 śarīravrttirvratam: Penance through bodily functions.

Although he is liberated from the body and bondage, he performs his bodily functions as acts of penance or worship to keep it alive.

3-27 kathā japah: His speech becomes japa:

The speech of the liberated yogi has the purity, sanctity and illumination of a sacred muttering.

3-28 dānam ātmajñānam: His teaching of self-knowledge is a gift.

The teaching of self-knowledge by the liberated yogi is a gift to the world.

3-29 yo'vipastho jñāhetuśca: He who is established in the avipa Shaktis is the cause of knowledge.

He who is established as the lord in the Avipa Shaktis who control the avis (beings in their animal state) is the cause of knowledge and the most qualified to gift the knowledge of Self.

3-30 svaśakti pracayo'sya viśvam: The universe is the outflow or expansion of his own Shaktis.

The universe is the outflow or expansion of his own Shaktis.

3-31 stithilayau: Preservation and destruction also.

Preservation and destruction are also filled with his Shaktis and illuminated by him only.

3-32 tat pravrttāvapyanirāsah samvettrbhāvāt: Even during such outward prvrittis, the state of the pure knower is unbroken.

3-33 sukha duhkhayorbahirmananam: Thinks that pain and pleasure are external.

His equanimity and self-knowing prevail because he thinks that dualities such as pain and pleasure are not happening to him, but external.

3-34 tadvimuktastu kevalī: Becoming free, he remains alone.

Becoming free thus from impurities, attachments, and dualities, he remains in oneness as Kevali.

3-35 mohapratisamhatastu karmātmā: The deluded one is verily karmatma.

The deluded one is verily a being of karma. He is produced by karma, made up of karma, guided and bound by karma.

3-36 bheda tiraskāre sargāntara karmatvam: Upon discarding the duality, the power to manifest another creation.

Upon discarding duality and division, the power to manifest another creation arises.

3-37 karanaśaktih svato'nubhavāt: Karana-shakti through self-experience.

From his own experience, the adept yogi realizes his karanashakti or the power to cause, create or manifest reality at will.

3-38 tripadādyanuprānanam: The three states are energized with prana by the first.

He also keeps energizing the three states of consciousness (wakeful, dream, and deep sleep) and the three states of activity (beginning, middle, and end), with the first, the bliss of turya or the memory of it.

3-39 cittasthitivat śarīra karana bāhyesu: As in the mind, so in the body, senses, and external objects.

Just as he fills his consciousness (chitta) with the fourth state of turya, so should he practice the same when his mind is externally engaged with his body, senses, and external objects.

3-40 abhilāsādbahirgatih samvāhyasya (sambahyasya): Due to desires the samvāhya is outbound.

Due to desires, the ignorant and deluded being (samvāhya) is outbound and moves among the sense objects of the world.

3-41 tadārūdhapramitestatkśayājjīvasamkśayah: Fixing the consciousness in it and removing desires, the jiva is dissolved.

Fixing his consciousness in the blissful fourth state of turya and suppressing desires, the yogi dissolves the jiva in him and, thereby, the limitedness and egoism which arise from it.

3-42 bhūtakañcukī tadā vimukto bhūyah patisamah parah: Then, freed from the gross and subtle, he becomes equal to the Supreme lord.

Then, freed from the influence and the limitations of gross and subtle bodies, he becomes free and equal to the supreme lord.

3-44 nāsikāntarmadhya samyamāt kimatra savyāpasavya sausumnesu: After controlling the breath in the middle of the nostrils, the left, right, and middle nadis, what else is to be done?

In the self-realized state, although freed from the limitations of jiva, the connection with prana remains natural, smooth, and flowing due to control and the purification of nerve channels (nadis).

3-45 bhūyah syāt pratimīlanam: There will be a reversal to the original state again.

With the illumination of the consciousness and dissolution of the beingness, the pure Self reverts to its original, pure state again.

Aum Tat Sat

Book Cover Credits

Front Cover Images: Adobe Stock, Asset IDs: #691279094 and #733159444
Back Cover Image: by visaxslr from Pixabay
Cover Design: V, Jayaram

www.ingramcontent.com/pod-product-compliance
Lightning Source LLC
Chambersburg PA
CBHW061328040426
42444CB00011B/2816